WHY GIVE "GIFTS" TO THE GIFTED?

investing in a national resource

LITA LINZER SCHWARTZ

CORWIN PRESS, INC.
A Sage Publications Company
Thousand Oaks, California

Copyright © 1994 by Corwin Press, Inc.

All rights reserved. No part of this book may be reproduced or utilized in any form or by any means, electronic or mechanical, including photocopying, recording, or by any information storage and retrieval system, without permission in writing from the publisher.

For information address:

Corwin Press, Inc.
A Sage Publications Company
2455 Teller Road
Thousand Oaks, California 91320

SAGE Publications Ltd.
6 Bonhill Street
London EC2A 4PU
United Kingdom

SAGE Publications India Pvt. Ltd.
M-32 Market
Greater Kailash I
New Delhi 110 048 India

Printed in the United States of America

Library of Congress Cataloging-in-Publication Data

Schwartz, Lita Linzer.
   Why give "gifts" to the gifted? : investing in a national resource / Lita Linzer Schwartz.
     p.   cm.
   Includes bibliographical references and index.
   ISBN 0-8039-6103-0.—ISBN 0-8039-6104-9 (pbk.)
   1. Gifted children—Education—United States.   I. Title.
LC3993.9.S39   1994
371.95′0973—dc20   93-40547

Cover design by Joshua D. Schwartz

94 95 96 97 98 10 9 8 7 6 5 4 3 2 1

Corwin Press Production Editor: Rebecca Holland

Contents

Preface	vii
Acknowledgments	ix
About the Author	x
1. Educating the Gifted: A National Resource	1
2. Identifying the Gifted	8
General Criteria	8
Types of Giftedness	11
Conclusion	20
3. Personal Qualities of the Gifted	21
Developing the Self: Concept and Identity	21
The Social Self	23
Difficulties and Dilemmas	24
Cognitive Traits and Learning Styles	26
Entering School	28
Leisure, Risk Taking, and Creativity	29
So Who Is the Gifted Individual?	31
4. The Underidentified Gifted	32
African Americans	35
Hispanics/Latinos	37
Asians and Pacific Islanders	40

Native Americans	41
Rural Students	44
Physically or Otherwise Handicapped	45
Students in Alternative Settings	46
Gifted Underachievers	49
Conclusion	52

5. Fostering Giftedness — 53
- Parental Role — 53
- The Role of Peers — 58
- Classroom Teachers — 59
- School Counselors — 62
- Community Attitude — 63

6. The Special Case of Gifted Females — 67
- "Are You a Girl or a Grind?" — 67
- Parents and Gifted Daughters — 69
- Gender-Specific Barriers — 70
- Effects of Giftedness on Nonacademic Life Areas — 76
- Counseling Gifted Girls — 78
- Conclusion — 80

7. Educational Options — 81
- Mainstreaming — 83
- Enrichment — 86
- Homogeneous Classes — 88
- Magnet Schools — 91
- Acceleration — 92
- Mentoring — 99
- Independent Study — 101
- Distance Education — 102
- Summer, Weekend, and Other Special Programs — 103
- Conclusion — 106

8. Follow-Up Studies — 107
- Terman's Study — 107
- Hunter High's Girls — 109
- The "Quiz Kids" — 111
- The Presidential Scholars — 112
- Study of Mathematically Precocious Youth (SMPY) — 113

St. Louis's Star Students	114
Gifted Youths in Israel	116
Lighthouse in Racine	116
Gifted at Ogontz	117
Conclusion	120
9. Conclusion	**122**
References	127
Name Index	143
Subject Index	148

Preface

The word "gift" has varying meanings according to the context in which it is used. The perfume given to a mother on Mother's Day is one kind of gift; a large sum of money given to a legislator by a lobbyist is another kind of gift; and the ability to create an inspiring piece of music is yet another type of gift. The motive underlying each of these gifts differs from love to bribery to inherent need for self-expression. We also give gifts to show our appreciation for someone's thoughtfulness, to enable a traveler to carry a memento of us while away, or to share in the joy of a bride and groom establishing a new life together. Our society deplores the bribery of legislators, but applauds the rest of these gifts.

The gifts of creativity, leadership, and the ability to manipulate words or numbers, however, are less concrete than packages in fancy paper with ribbons and may not be apparent until a "product" of some sort results. These gifts are *within* the individual and, like the seed of a plant, need advantageous conditions—nurturing—to develop, mature, and flower.

In what ways do we identify whose gifts we wish to encourage? Most often, the gifted are identified by intelligence test scores, but these are not and should not be the sole criteria used. For one thing, the abilities needed to succeed at a level markedly above average on tests and in the schoolroom form the basis of only one kind of gift. For another, too many individuals who are potentially able to succeed equally well are not so identified for a variety of reasons—lack of test-taking skills, test anxiety, lack of opportunity, or discouragement.

Many available texts deal with education of the gifted and talented, but I know of none that focuses on the "national resource" aspect of this population. Rather than describing a specific program for gifted and talented youth or providing strategies for teaching them, this book is aimed primarily at those who decide educational policy and which aspects of such policy will have financial support as well as administrative commitment.

The initial chapter establishes the basic premise that gifted and talented children represent a significant resource to any nation and it is profitable to the nation in many ways to invest in their healthy development and their education. Such an investment extends equal educational opportunity to them, just as legislation and public funding have provided such opportunity to other exceptional children.

Subsequent chapters describe types of giftedness, characteristics of gifted youth, underidentified gifted populations (and techniques for identifying them), and the role of adults in fostering giftedness and providing needed opportunities. One chapter is devoted to the special case of gifted females, because they have barriers to overcome that are typically not experienced by gifted, or even nongifted, boys, and parents and professionals alike should be aware of these problems. Of particular importance to decisionmakers is the chapter on options available for enhancing the educational experiences of gifted students, some of which cost virtually nothing and others of which may fly in the face of current practices. Nine categories of options and how these options can be modified and combined to meet the needs of a specific school district and its gifted students are included. A chapter on "follow-up" studies of gifted and talented students suggests certain commonalities in personal qualities among the "successful" gifted and talented as well as the kinds of activities that appear to promote achievement and maintain a positive self-concept. The concluding chapter ties these varied threads together and reaffirms the initial premise. The list of references is somewhat longer than it might ordinarily be so that readers can more quickly find sources that interest them.

All of this is basic but essential information for school board trustees, administrators, and legislators as they contemplate the long-term effects of their policy decisions.

Although the book is not a "how to" text for teachers of the gifted, it can also provide them with ideas and resources. As a thought-provoking book, it would thus be an appropriate supplemental text for college and university courses on education of the gifted and educational policy.

 # Acknowledgments

This book, like some others I've written, is the culmination of years of thought and experience. It owes a great deal to the encouragement I had from my late parents and from my brother, and to many teachers who were female models of competence. My young adult sons, Arthur, Joshua, and Frederic, can also take credit for opening my eyes to different kinds of gifts and talents and for helping me to develop some of my own in nonacademic areas.

There have been colleagues through the years, too, who have taught me much about the gifted and talented—in workshops, in conversation, and through their writings. Each of them has contributed, often unknowingly, to my thinking about the gifted and creative. Judy Featherman, a dear friend with her own expertise in the education of exceptional children, has shared both her knowledge and her editing ability as this book was being written.

Gracia A. Alkema, President of Corwin Press, has become a friend as well as publisher, and her prompt support of the ideas presented here was both welcome and a source of encouragement to push forward with their development.

Finally, for more than 15 years, I was given the freedom to explore in many directions and the opportunity to develop programs for the gifted and others at Penn State Ogontz by present and former Campus Executive Officers and Directors of Academic Affairs, as well as occasional funding support by The Pennsylvania State University for research studies. The staff of the Library at Penn State Ogontz have my greatest gratitude for all of the cooperation they have provided for so many years.

With the encouragement, teaching, and support of so many people, is it any wonder that there has been so much to mull over?

 About the Author

Lita Linzer Schwartz is Distinguished Professor of Educational Psychology and Professor of Women's Studies at Penn State's Ogontz Campus outside Philadelphia. A graduate of Vassar College, Temple University, and Bryn Mawr College, her dissertation focused on curiosity, anxiety, and intelligence in fifth graders. Her own curiosity has maintained interest in those and related areas, particularly emphasizing giftedness and creativity in females.

Schwartz has written texts for courses in Foundations of Education, Educational Psychology, and Education of Exceptional Children, as well as co-authoring a book on immigrant children and U.S. schools during the great immigration period of 1880-1920. In addition, she is co-author on a book on cults and conversion, co-author of a book on divorce, and most recently, author of the book *Alternatives to Infertility*. She has written articles or chapters in each of these areas, with special emphasis in recent years on legal and psychological ramifications of child custody contests arising from adoption and divorce. She is also a Fellow in the Divisions of Psychology and Law (41) and Family Psychology (43) in the American Psychological Association and holds a Diplomate in Forensic Psychology from the American Board of Professional Psychology (ABPP).

Although her interests may appear to be sharply diverse, she finds considerable overlap among them, as ultimately they all have an effect on children's self-image and behaviors. One of her principal concerns is that adults too often develop policies and practices that affect children without considering their long-term implications.

1 | Educating the Gifted: A National Resource

If, at age 5, you had just completed kindergarten and read with comprehension at a third-grade level, could add and subtract fractions "in your head," and had an advanced vocabulary, how exciting would you find the traditional first grade? Or, as a very bright secondary student, what might your alternatives be if your high school offered only 3 years of a foreign language and math only as far as trigonometry? Or, as may also be the case, what would happen if you were curious, good at problem solving, something of a risk taker, a leader among your peers, but bored in class and often sent to the office for disciplinary reasons?

We attend, quite justifiably, to the needs of the retarded, the learning disabled, the physically and sensorially handicapped, and the culturally different. However, too often the reaction to the needs of the gifted—the youths who should become the leaders of our nation in government, science, industry, education, and the arts—is that they can "make it on their own." However, many of them can't, or won't, "make it" on their own. They, too, need special programs and the support of their parents, their teachers, and the community if they are to try to work toward fulfilling their potential.

If, as a nation, we are truly committed to equal educational opportunity for all children, then special education for the gifted is not, as has been alleged, an elitist position. Indeed, according to Bull (1985), one of the principal arguments justifying special education for the gifted "is that these programs are necessary and appropriate ways to meet our currently unsatisfied *moral obligation* [italics added] to the precocious children for whom they are designed" (p. 2). In this era of concern with litigation regarding discrimination, might not the lack of appropriate education for the gifted be perceived as a wrong done and the basis for a suit against a school district?

2 ■ Why Give "Gifts" to the Gifted?

The gifted are by one definition as different from the "average" as are the mentally retarded. That is, on standardized intelligence tests they score two or more standard deviations above the mean, just as the retarded score two or more standard deviations below the mean. They should, like other exceptional students, have fully developed Individualized Education Programs (IEPs). This would encourage placement appropriate to their strengths and weaknesses as well as provide for their social and physical maturity levels. Well-prepared IEPs would be especially helpful for those (often identified) gifted students who also have specific learning deficits, and for those (usually unidentified) gifted who are at risk because of emotional or social adjustment problems. The same is true for those who are among the unidentified gifted because of their cultural or physical "differences." That there *are* indeed such unidentified gifted may come as a surprise to some, but I have worked with them, seen them perform at a level equal to that of their "identified" peers, and found substantial improvement a year later in their in-school behavior as well as their academic accomplishments (Schwartz & Fischman, 1984).

Newspaper headlines, magazine articles, and speakers at a wide variety of meetings deplore the low scores of U.S. students on standardized tests as compared with students in other countries. They deride the inadequate performance of U.S. workers and the loss of U.S. leadership in science and technology on the world stage. Changes *do* have to be made in our approach to education generally to rectify these problems, but changes also have to be made in attitudes toward educating gifted students specifically. As Gallagher (1988) wrote, the ambivalence that has characterized public attitudes toward education of the gifted must be changed if we are to move toward the national goal of educational excellence.

The primary argument against special education for the gifted is that it is undemocratic. Subthemes of this argument include the assertions that segregated schools for the gifted are elitist; that tracking has negative effects on those students not in the highest track (Does anyone really believe that first graders don't know that the "Robins" and the "Larks" are reading on different levels?); that acceleration is "bad" for the psychosocial and emotional development of the gifted; that such special programs discriminate against the children of minority groups; that these programs create morale problems between teachers of the gifted and teachers of other students; and, finally, that the programs are too expensive (especially in times of economic austerity). There is some truth to some of these assertions, depending on the specific setting, but these outcomes are neither universal nor unalterable. As so neatly described in the "Palcuzzi Ploy," such special programs have existed for gifted athletes in most communities for many years, with little objection from anyone except those who would prefer to see the emphasis placed on academics (Gallagher, 1975, pp. 83-84).

Almost 70 years ago, Lewis M. Terman (1925) opened the preface to his first volume of *Genetic Studies of Genius* with the following statement: "It should go without saying that a nation's resources of intellectual talent are among the most precious it will ever have" (p. vii). Zorbaugh and Boardman (1936) wrote a few years later:

> We, as a nation, are scandalously dissipating and wasting the resource represented by our gifted children. We spend annually millions on the feeble-minded, with no hope of return. Yet we are willing to invest little if anything in our gifted children, despite the fact that we might certainly expect an immeasurably rich return from such an investment. (p. 108)

Another leader in the study of the gifted, Leta S. Hollingworth, began a memorandum to the American Council on Education in the late 1930s with these words: "The development of all the world's natural resources depends on human intelligence, courage, stamina and will. It depends primarily on *thinking*. Therefore, intellectually gifted children are among the most valuable assets of a civilized nation. To waste them is to waste the fundamentals of power" (1940, p. 116).

In responding to arguments that special programs for the gifted are undemocratic, Gertrude Hildreth (1952), an educator of gifted children, wrote:

> It is unrealistic to insist that equal opportunity must always take the form of identical experience. Equal education for all children in a democracy must be interpreted as equivalent opportunity in terms of each child's needs and capacities.... By giving the gifted special training everyone will benefit from higher standards of living in the community, better government, better professional services. (p. 257)

Hildreth's recognition of "equivalent opportunity in terms of each child's needs and capacities" is the same rationale that underlies the Education for All Handicapped Children Act of 1975 (P.L. 94-142) and subsequent legislation in this field.

With the successful flight of the Soviet Union's Sputnik in October 1957, Congress quickly passed the National Defense Education Act of 1958, which stimulated and financially supported the development of a variety of programs in science, mathematics, and foreign languages—programs that attracted highly gifted students. After that flurry of activity, which lasted into the mid-1960s, public attitudes toward support of special education for the gifted again lapsed, with such efforts being termed antidemocratic and elitist (a word overused in this area).

More than two decades later, as public criticism of our entire educational system continued to increase, in 1989, President George Bush and the nation's governors (including then Governor Bill Clinton) met and developed a set of goals known as "Education 2000," the implementation of which was to correct the perceived weaknesses and outcomes of public education. As Gallagher (1988) had pointed out a year earlier,

> Once again . . . educational critics want to know what has happened to our goal of educational excellence. The truthful answer is that we have neither concentrated our own educational creativity nor committed sufficient resources to the task of educational program development for our top echelon of students—for two decades or more. We should not be surprised, therefore, at the limited number of high-quality programs for capable students. (p. 109)

Since then, we have seen a resurgence in calls for or attention to special programs for the gifted in both professional journals and the popular press.

The *Journal of Educational Psychology* devoted a substantial part of an issue to the education of the gifted, with the lead author repeating a now familiar refrain: "As a nation, we must guard against wasting the national resource that our gifted children represent" (Tomlinson-Keasey, 1990, p. 399). Extending that thought,

> Educators of the gifted are one voice, in what should be a chorus of voices, seeking to help citizens and policy makers alike understand that a school system which does not pursue excellence for all students (even those from whom we have traditionally expected little) as well as equity for all students (even those whom we have seen as "ahead of the game") is doomed to fail all students and the society which supports it. (Tomlinson & Callahan, 1992, p. 185)

That is, many of the techniques used to enhance learning for the gifted can be applied as well to the instruction of average students and may be modified to serve the less able, thus strengthening education for all. Indeed, as Gallagher (1986) asserted, "The curriculum reform of the 1960's, clearly aimed at the highest aptitude students, affected the curriculum for all students eventually" (p. 46). Does this not support the goals of "Education 2000"? Isn't this what we are clamoring for in demands for changes in school programs?

Bull (1985) also took this broader view, suggesting that we cannot always identify the potential contributors to society in their early years. Rather, he called for a "rigorous common curriculum for all students" and a program offering a variety of special experiences *for the education of gifts and talents*, not for the education of the gifted and talented [italics added]. These experiences should, he wrote, "(1) be numerous, diverse, and flexible; (2) provide for sustained involvement that leads to significant achievement for students; and (3) involve expert assistance, much of which may have to be drawn from outside the school" (p. 17). Such a perspective would perhaps permit the "unidentified" gifted and talented to experience the same kinds of challenges as their "identified" classmates, but it is at odds with curricula now in place in most schools. Until curricula attain the degree of rigor desired by Bull, there is considerable danger that those who have "gifts and talents" may become bored into a dislike of school or into behaviors that utilize their abilities in unacceptable ways.

One route to restoring excellence in education and national preeminence in a wide variety of fields of endeavor is to provide an appropriate education for gifted and talented students throughout their school years. Keep them interested in learning! Challenge them to solve problems! Help them to develop their gifts and their leadership abilities! Encourage them to share their techniques with peers and younger students who are not as well endowed! Techniques for providing appropriate opportunities even in regular (mainstream) classrooms are suggested by Mulhern (1978), Cox (1980), Levy (1981), Tucker (1982), and 25 additional authors in two volumes edited by R. M. Milgram (1989a, 1991a).

The U.S. Declaration of Independence asserts that "All men are created equal." As fine a philosophy as it is, in reality and in practice we know that the statement is untrue. It took a Supreme Court decision in 1954 to declare that "Separate but equal schools are inherently unequal." It took Congressional legislation in the 1960s and later to affirm that civil rights were being violated because of race; that individuals were being discriminated against because of gender, age, marital status; and that equality of educational *opportunity* did not exist for the handicapped and the disadvantaged. Fortunately, subsequent legislation provided statutory corrections.

The conflict between philosophy and practice is not unique to the United States. Consider, for example, the egalitarianism of the late Communist bloc, which posed a dilemma for policymakers in those countries. They were aware of the "link between developing the best minds of the young and furthering communist society" and "simultaneously hesitant to provide educational programs that might seem contrary to the notions of Marxist egalitarianism" (Mitchell & Williams, 1987, p. 533). Nevertheless, special programs, and sometimes special schools, were organized throughout the Soviet Union, in its satellite nations in Eastern Europe, and in the People's Republic of China. They provided advanced instruction for gifted and talented youth in the sciences, mathematics, visual and performing arts, and athletics.

Despite fears that special education for the gifted and talented might be seen as a form of elitism and privilege,

> most nations see the necessity of nurturing their best minds and talents. National progress—in some cases, even national survival—is strongly linked to identifying gifted and talented young people and providing special educational programs for them. . . . Coupled with the desire for national progress and development is a realization, in most nations, that comprehensive systems of mass education tend to stifle the development of gifted or talented students. (Mitchell & Williams, 1987, p. 534)

In November 1993, the U.S. Department of Education released a study on gifted children, its first in two decades, adding its voice in favor of differential education for the gifted as well as urging greater efforts to identify gifted and talented children in minority groups (Jordan, 1993).

Equality of educational opportunity does not mean that all students should be treated equally in our schools. Indeed, many school administrators, particularly in relatively affluent school districts, proudly assert that each student in their schools is taught in the way most appropriate for him or her (although in practice this may not be quite true). If this were an accurate statement, the school curriculum and the progress of gifted students through the schools would be modified appropriately to meet these students' needs and abilities, using one or more of the options to be discussed later in this book. As R. M. Milgram (1992) stated, "Equal educational opportunity is a presumed value in many societies. When we provide the same education to gifted and nongifted learners, we are in effect not providing the gifted with equal opportunity" (p. 246). Or, as Monks (1991) put it, "Gifted children and prodigies do not need more or a better treatment, but a different treatment" (p. 13).

As so many have said over the course of so many decades, and as so many governments of varying philosophies have demonstrated in action, an investment in the present and the future of the gifted is an investment in the nation's future. Something seems seriously askew, however, when the same arguments are presented over a more than 50-year period and inadequate programming still prevails. Can all of those I have quoted be in error?

2 Identifying the Gifted

In 1979, it was estimated that there were 2.5 million gifted children in the United States with IQ scores that exceeded 130 and whose ranks included "music, math, and chess prodigies; budding poets, ballerinas, and basketball stars" (Bentsen, 1979, p. 36). This count in a popular magazine article did not even include those who had not been identified by high IQ scores, but was meant to alert the residents of New York City to the needs of children whose abilities (or potential) were not being met except through the prodigious efforts of their parents and a few special school programs.

In some cases, as with the extremely gifted and talented Bentsen described, formal "identification" is not needed because the child's gifts or talents are apparent as early as one year of age. More often, however, school systems use standardized tests, and, increasingly, other mechanisms to find these youngsters and provide them with the educational services appropriate to their abilities. It is important, indeed essential, to recognize, however, that gifted students with similar scores do not necessarily have similar specific abilities and needs or benefit from identical programming. Gifted and talented students are as unique in their patterns of strengths and weaknesses as any other youngsters.

General Criteria

The standard definition used in identifying exceptionally able students is the one included in the Gifted and Talented Children's Act of 1978 (Education Amendments of 1978, P.L. 95-561, Title IX):

Gifted and talented children means children, and whenever applicable, youth, who are identified at the preschool, elementary, or secondary level as possessing demonstrated or potential abilities that give evidence of high performance capability in areas such as intellectual, creative, specific academic, or leadership ability, or in the performing or visual arts, and who by reason thereof require services or activities not ordinarily provided by the school. (*Congressional Record*, 1978, p. H-12179)

There are also those who are gifted in the psychomotor area, being unusually well coordinated and capable of athletic feats such as world-class figure skating or remarkably able in basketball or other physical tasks requiring a combination of dexterity, intellectual ability, and sensory acuity.

Tannenbaum (1983) takes particular notice of the *potential* of giftedness, proposing a future-oriented definition: "*It denotes their potential for becoming critically acclaimed performers or exemplary producers of ideas in spheres of activity that enhance the moral, physical, emotional, social, intellectual, or aesthetic life of humanity* [italics in the original]" (p. 86). As with others in this field, he sees "excellence" as an effect of the interaction of several factors: general ability, special ability, environmental factors, nonintellective factors, and chance factors. There is likely to be less quarrel with this five-factor model than with Tannenbaum's use of the word "enhance" as an essential element of his definition. He deliberately excludes from qualifying as gifted "those who can do no better than consume and appreciate ideas, even though they score well on familiar measures of mastery and constitute the best known pool from which the gifted are most likely to be located" (p. 422). His objection to including people in the community of "the gifted" who use their abilities for destructive purposes is included in the discussion of "social" giftedness below.

Although the most common identifier of the gifted is the score on an individual IQ test, it is not the only instrument available nor is it appropriate for all students. In Renzulli's view (Renzulli & Reis, 1991), giftedness is present when there is *interaction* among Above Average Ability, Task Commitment, and Creativity (see Figure 2.1). In addition, giftedness occurs in certain people under certain circumstances at certain times. In other words, not everyone identified as "gifted" performs at that level at all times. Gifted performance requires some interest in the activity at hand, and interest, for Renzulli, requires opportunities, resources, and encouragement. It should be noted that opportunity includes the existence of an avenue to demonstrate the gift or talent. For example, Midori could not be a

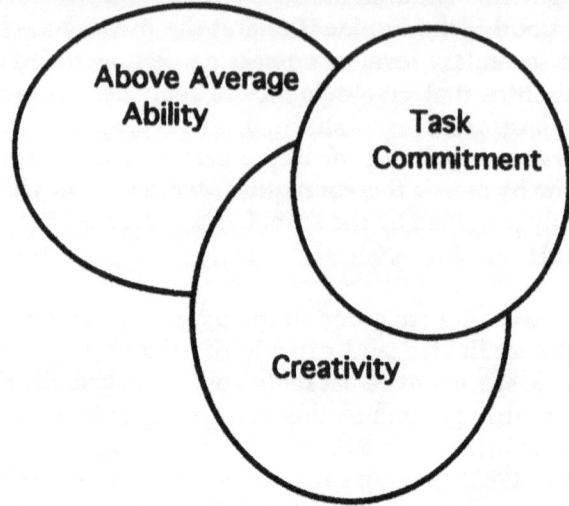

Figure 2.1. Elements of Giftedness (after Renzulli & Reis, 1991)

gifted violinist if the violin had not yet been invented (D. Feldman, 1986; Tannenbaum, 1992).

Schack and Starko (1990) found differences among pre-service teachers, experienced classroom teachers, and teachers of the gifted on the criteria they suggested for selecting students for gifted programs. Creativity was the criterion most frequently chosen by teachers in all groups, but novices as well as experienced teachers tended to focus more on grades and classroom performance than did teachers of the gifted. The latter group, by contrast, focused more on criteria such as vocabulary (generally considered the best single indicator of intelligence), multiplicity of interests, ability to learn "quickly and easily," *and* IQ scores. This suggested to the researchers, as it should to others, the need to teach multimodal assessment to prospective and in-service teachers.

For an example, educators should examine the Gifted Evaluation Scale (McCarney, 1987). This 48-item scale, which covers IQ score in one question, asks the rater to evaluate the student on a scale of 1 to 5 ("Does not demonstrate the behavior or skill" to "Demonstrates the behavior or skill at all times [consistently]") on items that cover five subscale areas: Intellectual, Creativity, Specific Academic Aptitude, Leadership Ability, and Performing and Visual Arts. The raw scores are then translated into standard scores and percentiles. Evaluators—whether teachers or counselors—are urged, first, to be familiar with the child they are rating, and second, to take their time (e.g., several hours over a period of days) in completing the form so that they have as accurate a picture of the child as possible.

Other ways of identifying the gifted include examination of a student portfolio (in visual arts, in use of language, etc.), nomination by teacher specialists or librarians, or the use of a structured interview (based perhaps on self- or teacher nomination). It is increasingly apparent that multimodal assessment is more desirable because it is a more effective identifier of gifted youths than a single IQ score. These assessments are discussed more fully in the next several pages.

Types of Giftedness

When the average person thinks of "the gifted," it is usually, as already noted, within the context of academic intelligence as measured by standardized IQ tests. This is certainly one legitimate perception. However, as Kornhaber, Krechevsky, and Gardner (1990) have asserted, in practice intelligence is a

> manifestation of engagements between two components: (a) individuals, who are capable of using their array of competences in various domains of knowledge; and (b) the societies that foster individual development through the opportunities they provide, the institutions they support, and the value systems they promote. Individual competences represent only one aspect of intelligence; intelligence also requires social structures and institutions that enable the development of these competences. (p. 182)

This, in a way, is an expansion of Lewin's (1954) definition of behavior as a function of the interaction of the person and the environment. (See p. 27 for a fuller discussion of this perspective.) Rather than looking at the immediate field in which the individual functions, Kornhaber et al. consider the global context. Translated into sociopolitical phenomena, one might consider whether a high level of social intelligence (interpersonal competence in Gardner's terminology) is valued and encouraged in a totalitarian society or a truly communal society, just as one might question whether perfect musical pitch is valued or encouraged in a subgroup composed of severely hearing-impaired people versus a subgroup of people with normal hearing ability, or in another context, whether the brilliance of a Latin scholar will be regarded as giftedness in a nontechnological culture that depends upon (and therefore values highly) psychomotor skills for survival.

Bull (1985) states this proposition in another, but clearly related way: "If . . . a conception of giftedness is to serve as a predictor of cultural eminence it must . . . be attuned to the precise opportunities for revolutionary cultural innovation that exist at a particular time and place and, consequently, the precise configurations of skill and inclination necessary to exploit those opportunities" (p. 6). Further, after a brief review of Einstein's early struggles to explain electromagnetism, Bull restates the proposition: "Einstein's history suggests that . . . eminence arises from the coincidence of cultural opportunities and individuals with the specific abilities to take advantage of them *not*, as our current conceptions of giftedness seem to imply, from certain general and timeless forms of individual genius" (p. 7). In other words, Einstein's genius might not have been as evident if Isaac Newton had not made his contributions to physics centuries earlier. This is the very point that D. Feldman (1986) and Tannenbaum (1992) were making. There is a vital interactive quality that is the underpinning, as it were, of behavior and transcends the individual's genetic makeup and specific environment.

As Kornhaber et al. (1990) also suggest, it must be recognized that different competencies develop at varying rates and need more or less instruction. Gardner (1983) identified seven areas of competence: linguistic, musical, logical-mathematical, spatial, bodily kinesthetic, interpersonal, and intrapersonal: "Each competence has a developmental trajectory relatively independent of the others. . . . The relative strengths of the seven competences vary within and among individuals to form different 'profiles'" (p. 183). (Note that in fact any observant parent can tell you that children's abilities similarly develop on individual schedules, so that for one period of time, all progress appears to be in the psychomotor area, but then that slows and verbal ability grows by leaps and bounds, and so on.)

The concept of individual profiles that reflect intrapersonal strengths and weaknesses had, of course, also been propounded by Thurstone (1938). His test of Primary Mental Abilities, however, had stressed principally academic-type skills, such as verbal comprehension, memory, spatial ability, numerical reasoning, and the like. The test did not, unlike the Stanford-Binet, the Wechsler series, and other tests of intelligence, yield a single overall "IQ," but rather a profile of the individual's abilities.

Sternberg (1990) sought to evaluate the individual in practical contexts as well as the more traditional ones. His Triarchic Abilities

Test "also seeks to measure another aspect of intelligence: the abilities to cope with novelty and to automatize information processing" (p. 215). Thus, those identified as "gifted" might be seen as more creative as well because they are able to apply what they know in diverse ways.

Yet another approach that seeks to move beyond giftedness as solely related to an IQ score is Milgram's 4×4 Structure of Giftedness model (R. M. Milgram, 1989b). Two of her four categories are concerned with aspects of intelligence (general intellectual ability and specific intellectual ability) and the other two "with aspects of original thinking (general original/creative thinking and specific creative talent)" (p. 10). Drawn as a cube, one dimension deals with these four categories or types of ability; a second dimension deals with levels, from nongifted to profoundly gifted; and the third dimension deals with settings—home, school, and community. The cube itself is "embedded in a solid circle of individual differences associated with age, sex, socioeconomic status, culture, subculture, and personality characteristics (e.g., task commitment, learning style, and autonomy)" (p. 11). This conception has strong ties to the Lewinian perspective of a "field" in which the individual operates, but is more explicit. In addition, Milgram's perception of the importance of leisure activities in the life of the gifted child is very much in accord with multimodal assessment techniques that include self-nomination and parent nomination as means of locating previously unidentified gifted youths.

In the view of Feldhusen, Asher, and Hoover (1984), "A sound identification process includes five major steps, each of which must be viewed separately in order to determine its validity within the framework of the entire process" (p. 149). They identify these steps as:

1. The clarification of the goals of the identification process and the program, including the types of youth to be served.
2. The application of a nomination-screening process that uses appropriate and psychometrically sound measures.
3. The use of assessment procedures that reduce the number of youths to be served and that "yield diagnostic information about the student's special talents, aptitudes, abilities, strengths, weaknesses, and needs" (p. 150).
4. The differentiation of individuals for the differentiation of education.
5. The validation of the identification process through correlation of the measures used with criteria of success in the gifted program.

To these, Birch (1984) added that psychoeducational assessment should begin, if possible, before the child enters school. In addition, he would "Instruct parents, teachers, principals, librarians, physicians, counselors, supervisors, and other significant adults in what to look for to help them spot gifted children and youth at home, in school and in the community" (p. 160).

Academic Giftedness

Numerous studies of the academically gifted have identified several characteristics of youths in this group. They tend to have above-average abstract thinking and reasoning abilities, an advanced vocabulary (often the initial clue to a child's intellect), a well-developed memory, accelerated reading skills, a wide range of information, strong task commitment, the ability to think through complex problems, and alternative ways of dealing with their environment. In addition, many of the cognitively gifted prefer to work independently, finding their own ways to solve problems.

The most common way of identifying academically gifted students is through individual testing on a Binet or Wechsler scale of intelligence, with a 130 IQ as the usual lower limit. In the years when the Stanford-Binet test used the simple Mental Age/Chronological Age = IQ formula, it was theoretically possible for particularly a young gifted child to score above 200 IQ (e.g., MA = 125, CA = 60, $\therefore$ IQ = 208). The more recent use of age-related standard deviation-based tables for each subtest, especially on the Wechsler Preschool and Primary Scale of Intelligence-Revised, however, appears to pose some limitations for the brightest preschoolers and possibly for extremely bright older subjects as well. The concern is principally with the "limitations on the amount of subtest *variability* that can be displayed by the brightest children" (Kaplan, 1992, p. 406).

The highly gifted, those who score three or more standard deviations above the mean (IQ 145+), frequently teach themselves a wide variety of skills such as reading or mathematics while still in the preschool years and may have an unusual level of sophistication for their age. They often demonstrate exceptional problem-solving skills, but cannot explain how they reached a solution. They may also be precocious in motor development and unusually mature about moral issues (Hollingworth, 1942; Silverman, 1989). These characteristics make it difficult for them to interact optimally with their agemates or even most of their caretakers or teachers.

Child prodigies, as highly gifted preschoolers are frequently labeled, are not necessarily doomed to early burnout or emotional breakdowns in adulthood, as some "horror stories" would have everyone believe. But these children also should not be exploited, as has been the case in the past (and occasionally even today). D. Feldman (1986), Radford (1990), and Tannenbaum (1992) reviewed the histories of a number of such prodigies. One message that comes through is that they are children, deserving of and needing tender loving care as much as any other child. Instructive and perhaps challenging stimulation as well as high-level parent-child verbal interaction within a nurturing environment appear to lay a good foundation for preschool prodigies to develop into gifted and reasonably healthy adults (Tannenbaum, 1992). On the other hand, the intensive training fostered by some parents of prodigies can be both exploitative and abusive, and overprotection is as unhealthy for these youngsters as for any others. We have only to think of some of the very talented young athletes, perhaps especially the gymnasts aged 10 or 11, who have spent their entire childhood preparing for a few moments of glory in the Olympics, squeezing traditional education between stretches of practice time and having no time for being a child, but only a cozened national (or family) symbol.

Another perception regarding child prodigies is that their development tends to be uneven (e.g., cognitive compared with psychomotor development), possibly even "lurching" at times, as when a nonspeaker at age 2 suddenly breaks into lengthy utterances with advanced vocabulary. A gift for languages is one of the abilities seen in some prodigies (John Stuart Mill, for example); remarkable musical talent (as in Mozart's case) is another.

Like several others who have developed programs for gifted students, Renzulli (1984) believes that identification of the gifted should be multidimensional, because these children exhibit their abilities in more than one way. He allows also for both cultural differences (by including culturally sensitive evaluators) and freedom of expression (i.e., a greater flexibility) in response. Renzulli and his associates identify what they call the "Talent Pool" of the top 15%-20% of the school population and include most of these students in curriculum modifications and enrichment activities. Their rationale "is that, by definition, students working at the 80th or 85th percentile are clearly capable of showing high degrees of mastery of the regular curriculum" (p. 165). As he points out, however, the final size of a Talent Pool in a given school may depend upon the needs of particular school populations as well as the availability and resources of the teachers and administration in that school.

In keeping with this philosophy, selection for the Talent Pool is based on several sources:

Psychometric Information is derived from traditional tests of intelligence, aptitude, achievement, and creativity. *Developmental Information* is obtained through the use of teacher, parent, and self-nomination and rating scales. *Sociometric Information* is derived from peer nominations and ratings and *Performance Information* is based on actual examples of previous accomplishments in school and non-school settings.... A "safety valve," entitled Special Nominations, is also used as a final check to help minimize the chances of excluding potential Talent Pool members who might have been overlooked in the final steps of the process. (p. 165)

The result of this multifaceted selection process is that there are larger numbers of students receiving, and profiting from, a variety of special services. The effects of inclusion will be discussed in a later chapter.

Heid (1983) enumerated behaviors in the mathematically gifted that go beyond those usually associated with the gifted. These include the ability to reason through mathematical problems without going through every step (also known as *curtailment* or *abbreviated reasoning*), "quick and comprehensive generalization" in problem solving, problem solving in the abstract rather than the concrete, and an "inclination to analyze the mathematical structure" of a problem rather than deal with its specific details (pp. 222-223). These youths also seem to have flexibility in thinking, a behavior that is shared with many other gifted students, as well as with those labeled creative. All of these abilities and behaviors, according to Heid, demand a nontraditional mathematics curriculum, one that will allow these particular gifted children to work independently and at length at tasks of which they apparently never tire—doing mathematics. They can be encouraged to develop multiple approaches and solutions to problems rather than just one.

Sometimes the giftedness is even more focused, as in Frydman and Lynn's (1992) study of Belgian children aged 8-13 years who were gifted chess players. Although their chess playing was of exceptional quality, on average the three groups of children ($N = 33$) would not have qualified as gifted on either Verbal or Full-Scale IQ scores. Their Performance IQs, however, reflected their strong visual-spatial abilities, which, combined with above-average intelligence, apparently contributed to their success in playing chess. The strength of their nonverbal abilities relative to their verbal skills should suggest that they, like other gifted youth, would profit from alternative instructional strategies as well as the more traditional modes.

In addition to the characteristics already discussed, many of the cognitively gifted also have a wide-ranging curiosity, which may or may not engender a positive response from the significant adults around them. Too often, the child's constant "Why?" evokes the impatient reply of "You ask too many questions!" "Thus, the teacher who 'turns on' the child's curiosity is . . . remembered long afterward as part of a pivotal educational event" (Baska, 1989, p. 19).

Social Intelligence

In looking for those who are "socially" intelligent, we are following the lead of Edward L. Thorndike (1920), who hypothesized three kinds of intelligence: social, abstract, and concrete. A person scoring high in social intelligence would be able to understand people's motivations, perceive social relationships, be sensitive to others' feelings, comprehend everyday problems, and generally get along well with others. A child or adult with these abilities could be a very effective leader.

Such an individual may or may not also be gifted in abstract (generally perceived as academic) or concrete (object-oriented or mechanical) intelligence. Although those gifted in social intelligence could be highly successful as adults in fields such as sales, public relations, or mental health, Thorndike foresaw difficulties for them in the basic education sector if they do not also have average or better abstract intelligence.

How can the socially gifted be identified? As with other kinds of intelligence, a multimodal approach seems to be most desirable. Self-nomination, peer nomination, teacher nomination, personality questionnaires, and biographical data including examples of leadership in extracurricular activities are among the screening instruments commonly used (Karnes & Meriweather-Bean, 1991). The socially gifted often share characteristics with those identified as academically gifted or creative, such as being independent, exercising initiative, being a good planner, being innovative, assuming responsibility beyond what might be expected based on age, and being able to bring others together in an harmonious way.

There is an assumption on the part of researchers that the socially gifted have a high level of moral reasoning and behave in a prosocial manner, thus excluding such leaders as Hitler and Jim Jones from consideration (Abroms, 1985). It should be noted, however, that these figures demonstrated their sensitivity to what makes others "tick" and knew how to manipulate people's needs and desires very effectively. Such an *anti*social application of social intelligence can be equally effective in more individualized negative settings, as when a gifted youth drops out of school because of boredom or frustration and joins a delinquent peer group. The task here is to help the socially gifted to use their "relational skills" in constructive ways.

Artistic Gifts

Identifying the child gifted in visual arts frequently does not occur until secondary school. Chetelat (1981), an art teacher at the elementary level who believed that it was important for such identification to happen earlier, used his own observations of children in art class, nominations (from an art teacher, parent, child, or child's peer), and an artwork portfolio to find such youngsters. Because they were attending the usual elementary-level art class with their peers, he made use of learning station experiences to challenge those who were artistically talented. He also had them develop art demonstrations, sometimes in conjunction with average students, and encouraged their participation in community art enrichment activities.

Those gifted in music are often identified by an unusual sense of pitch or a thrillingly clear singing voice at an early age. They may sit down at the piano keyboard and almost flawlessly pick out a melody just heard on the radio, possibly elaborating on it as they play it a second time, or like the child Mozart, they may play what they hear in their "inner ear."

Gifted dancers-to-be may be identified by the fluidity of their movement in formal classes or less structured settings. Female gymnasts, typically peaking in their preadolescent years, are also identified early. Those who will star as actors or entertainers more often emerge in the middle or secondary school years when opportunities for performance increase.

Although larger schools and school districts may be willing and able to provide supportive instruction or extracurricular activities for these gifted children, more often the parents must seek appropriate learning activities elsewhere in the community for their children. Adaptation to the needs of the artistically gifted and talented is thus more typically one of adjusting time schedules for extended practice rather than of altering course content (except in their area of expertise, of course). Although appropriate educational opportunities should be available for them, somewhat less attention will be paid to their needs as gifted/talented children in these pages than to the needs of the academically gifted.

Creativity

The criteria for labeling ideas and products "creative" include fluency, flexibility, elaboration, and originality (Torrance, 1966). Virtually everyone has the potential for thinking creatively, but traditional curricula tend to focus on *con*vergent thinking (one correct answer) rather than *di*vergent thinking (many "correct" answers), which somewhat stifles creative thinking. Related to creative thinking is problem-solving ability, in which the first task may be to identify the problem, followed by fact finding, idea generation, identification of possible solutions, and evaluation of the solutions. All of these abilities can be taught to all students, but as Fishkin (1993) pointed out, "Our brightest youngsters are capable of becoming creative producers, rather than merely consumers of existing information. Thus, increasing their skill in developing unique solutions to real problems is an important goal for educators of the gifted" (p. 7).

One problem that Torrance (1984) pointed out, however, relative to identifying and developing creative abilities, "is that of dealing with a national climate that is generally unfavorable to creative achievement. This is further complicated by a national climate that rather generally discourages the full development of potentialities, except for certain types of athletics" (p. 153). Bitter as this may sound, it merely restates what Gallagher said in the "Palcuzzi Ploy" (1975) mentioned in the first chapter.

The assessment of creative thinking ability, as differentiated from measures of intellectual ability, is effectively reviewed by Runco (1992). He examines the theories underlying the principal approaches; the nature and scoring of tests for creative thinking; and factors affecting children's performance on these tests, such as age, personality traits, incentives, models, and so on. He concludes that "these tests provide *useful* estimates of the *potential* for creative thinking" (p. 257).

In a study with intermediate school gifted, talented, and nongifted youngsters, Runco (1986) gave standard instructions and explicit instructions to "be creative" and "give only original responses." The children also completed a creative accomplishment self-report in which they indicated the quantity and quality of their extracurricular activity in seven performance areas. On all 15 subtests (five each for fluency, flexibility, and originality), the gifted sample had higher mean scores than either of the other groups. Interestingly, though, "for all children, fluency and flexibility scores were higher in the standard instructions than in the explicit instructions condition, and the originality scores were higher in the explicit instructions than in the standard instructions condition" (p. 312). He concluded that "gifted children differ quite substantially from nongifted children in their perceptions of divergent thinking tasks, and we might infer that extra-cognitive ability is an important aspect of giftedness" (p. 313).

In another facet of the same study, Runco and Albert (1986) found that "the divergent thinking of exceptionally gifted adolescent boys, unlike that of nongifted individuals, is associated with the divergent thinking of their parents" (pp. 342-343). They suggest a number of factors that might explain this relationship, but one that should suggest itself to parents in particular is the possibility that the behavior they present, the searching for multiple solutions or answers, is a meaningful model to their children.

The nontraditional thinking of creative students may be erroneously perceived by some school personnel as evidence of psychopathology rather than talent. A sample of 72 gifted students 11 to 16 years old (IQ >135) and comparison groups was given the Rorschach Inkblot Test by Gallucci (1989), and a Child Behavior Checklist was completed by their teachers. The gifted students had a higher frequency of responses on the Rorschach that were nonentrenched, intellectually sophisticated, and "odd" or "peculiar" than their nongifted peers. These differences, however, did not indicate psychopathology, although "72% (65 of 90) of the cases in the entire gifted sample were falsely identified as positive for schizophrenia" (p. 757). The scores on the behavior checklist did not support such diagnoses.

Treffinger (1986) pointed out that some techniques fostering creativity can be taught to students at all ability levels (e.g., brainstorming, attribute listing, making inferences), whereas applying these "basic tools" to group problem solving and to real-world problems may require a higher level of ability. Creative problem solving, after all, is partially dependent upon the breadth and depth of information relevant to the problem that the problem solver brings to the task.

Conclusion

Giftedness appears in many guises. The most obvious and most familiar form is intellectual ability, usually expressed in an IQ score, but occasionally by grade point average (GPA) in secondary school or higher education. Possibly combined with above-average academic ability, but also possibly standing alone, are social giftedness, artistic talent, and creativity. These gifts appear at different ages, under varying circumstances, and with differing degrees of acceptance.

I have already noted that every individual is unique, and this is as true of the gifted as of everyone else. There are some characteristics that most gifted people share, however, and a discussion of the personal qualities of the gifted is the focus of the next chapter.

3 Personal Qualities of the Gifted

When you think of the characteristics of U.S. heroes over the nation's history, what pops into mind? A strategist might think of a military or political leader's ability to look at the "big picture"; someone else might recall the dogged persistence of the pioneers who went West into killer blizzards, Indian wars, and other hazards—and still others might honor the heroism and persistence of the Indians; and a romantic might mention Horatio Alger's young heroes who "made it" because a mentor perceived their talents and invested time, energy, and sometimes money into their development. In more recent years, we have lauded those who conceived of the idea and put astronauts on the moon, the astronauts themselves, those who not only developed but then miniaturized the computer, and those who have been leaders in a wide variety of altruistic enterprises. All of these figures had some qualities that set them apart from most of their peers. Sometimes their nontraditional preferences and characteristics brought them into conflict with the "establishment," but they tended to pursue their goals nevertheless, whether on the frontiers of the West or of space or in the laboratory. What is it that distinguishes these heroes (gifted individuals) from their peers?

Developing the Self: Concept and Identity

Erikson (1960) pointed out that the elementary school years call for feelings of industry/achievement (with feelings of inferiority at the other end of the continuum) and the adolescent years for finding one's identity (with role confusion as its antithesis). As the adolescent moves toward young adulthood, the extremes of the continuum are intimacy and isolation. Actually, these stages tend to overlap rather than adhere to rigid age groups, so that the individual seeks to achieve *and* to "find" him/herself, *and* to develop close relationships with peers concurrently. For the gifted child or adolescent, this often means confrontation in the school years with difficult choices, especially those relating to peer relationships.

Seeking and establishing an identity is as important a task for these youths as for any others. The gifted tend to have more imagination, offering them more opportunities to experiment with identities than most of their peers have. Halsted (1988) suggested, with some justification, that reading books offers "possibilities they would otherwise not encounter and permit[s] them to experience vicariously various roles and ways of living as they move through the process of creating a personal identity" (pp. 5-6). Their imaginations are enriched by the biographies, histories, and fiction they read, and the more visually oriented among them can "see" themselves in a wide range of settings and roles.

Some may assume that the intellectually gifted child or adolescent has such a strong self-concept that he or she may at times be regarded as smug or a "know-it-all." At the very least, unknowing adults may take for granted that the gifted youth has a positive self-concept, but this is not always true. Is the self-concept of gifted youths similar to or different from that of average youths? Studies on self-concept of the gifted have yielded contradictory results over the years, with Terman, for example, finding that his gifted subjects tended to be better adjusted than their average peers, whereas Hollingworth suggested that those in the highest IQ groups might indeed have social and emotional adjustment problems (Grossberg & Cornell, 1988; Hollingworth, 1942). Grossberg and Cornell, incidentally, found no support for Hollingworth's view in their own study of gifted elementary students (aged 7 to 11 years); their analysis supported Terman's perspective.

Self-concept involves a number of components: cognitive, physical, social, athletic, appearance, and global, for example. Each of these areas is scored on The Self-Perception Profile for Children, which was used with gifted youngsters in Grades 5-8 who were in enrichment classes (Hoge & McSheffrey, 1991). Scholastic or cognitive self-concept seemed generally to contribute more weight to "global self-concept" than other subfactors; Hoge and McSheffrey found no significant differences between the sexes on global self-concept at any grade level, suggesting to them that "enrichment education may have a particularly beneficial effect for girls" (p. 241).

One study of 13-year-old white middle-class eighth graders, both gifted and average, suggests that the two groups are more similar in self-concept than different (Yong & McIntyre, 1991). The only significant difference noted on the Piers-Harris Children's Self-Concept Scale was in the area of "behavior," where the gifted group had a higher mean score than the average group. This suggested to the authors, even as they recommended replication with a larger sample, "that the students identified as gifted tended to be more positive about themselves as persons and about their ability to communicate interpersonally at home and school than their regular peers" (p. 445).

If gifted black students are questioned, however, the responses may be quite different. Ford, Harris, and Schuerger (1993) found defense mechanisms of denial and projection at work in the students, as well as ambivalence toward themselves, their peers, and whites with whom they might interact as teachers and counselors. The needs for appropriate role models and for increasing multiethnic sensitivity on both sides are evident if the gifted black child, in this case, or other minority child, is to see beyond present dilemmas and achieve in keeping with ability.

The Social Self

Typically, the gifted child, even in the preschool years, is advanced in social maturity as well as in specific areas of competence. Gifted children tend also to be high achievers, but this may well put them in line for peer disapproval, rejection, or ostracism. Thus, "if the urge to achieve is positively influenced by socialization, it might equally be quashed by social pressures to reduce one's drive or productivity. If so, the gifted student who is subjected to intense and continual pressure to moderate his performance might eventually lose his motivation to succeed" (Gross, 1989, p. 191).

Young gifted children may even have some difficulty relating to their peers at the nursery school level, for they often have different play interests from their age peers. On the other hand, they may have more acute sensitivity to other people's feelings and a more sophisticated sense of humor than the usual preschooler. They tend to have more vivid imaginations and to prefer games involving ideas and strategies more than simply rigid rules (Gross, 1989). In addition, they may have a drive for perfection that can either be strongly motivating or that may inhibit risk taking (Perez, 1980). If the teacher downplays the child's abilities in order to obtain conformity in the group, there will be a negative impact on the child's self-concept.

Most high-ability students have good social skills and greater social maturity than their age peers, enabling them to get along well and be comfortable with both their peers and those a few years older. In a study of 319 gifted students in Grades 5-11 participating in a 2-week residential summer enrichment program at the University of Virginia, however, peer nominations and peer ratings identified a group that clearly had peer relations problems (Cornell, 1990). Comparison of these unpopular students with average and popular peers revealed statistical differences in academic achievement, academic self-concept, or family social status only in one item: Significant differences were found in father's occupation, with fathers of the least popular children having a much less prestigious occupation than those in the average and popular groups. Perhaps more important, the least popular group had significantly lower scores on social self-concept ($p < .01$) and on social attraction ($p < .01$) and rated themselves lower in initiative, social attention, and success/failure (all at $p < .05$) on questionnaires focused on self-competence, emotional autonomy, and anxiety. Teachers also noted these youths' inappropriate or unassertive behavior in the classroom. The causes for the negative self-perceptions and less than desirable behaviors were unclear, but do suggest the need to help unpopular students, average as well as gifted, gain appropriate social skills.

Difficulties and Dilemmas

Although gifted students may have a very positive self-concept as related to academic or other achievement, the result is often the antithesis in social acceptance. As Gross (1989) and others have suggested, peer disapproval may lead the gifted student to become the class clown or the leader in mischief to gain approval. Indeed, among peers who devalue education altogether, giftedness might even be literally hazardous to a child's continued existence—unless the talents are turned away from the academic and toward the asocial goals of the gang. This leads to a pattern of "fear of success" because the price of successful achievement is very dear—loss of peer acceptance and approval.

This dilemma seems to afflict the extremely gifted more than the moderately gifted because the latter tend to be more able to find some common interests with their age peers. There must, therefore, be more opportunities for the extremely able to establish positive peer relations. Special classes, workshops, or schools that give them a chance to interact with each other appear to enhance their personal and social adjustment as well as provide intellectual stimulation. Robinson and Janos (1986), for example, found that radically accelerated students did not differ significantly in psychosocial adjustment from National Merit Scholars or from their college classmates who were a few years older, and "appeared somewhat less alienated from peers than did normal-aged college students" (p. 58).

Another difficulty that can arise is a fear of failure. The gifted or talented youth is accustomed to performing perfectly and often expected to do so, or very nearly, but may become so afraid at some point of not performing at the usual level that he or she withdraws from activity. Nadia Salerno-Sonnenberg (1993), a gifted violinist, related in an interview her memories of such a fear of failure in her late teens and early 20s, although she had made a very successful debut at age 10 with the Philadelphia Orchestra. The questions besetting her were "Can I do it again?" and "Was that a fluke?" Others are troubled by a similar fear as they move into more competitive schools or programs where their classmates are equally gifted and the assignments are more challenging. Indeed, for gifted students from isolated settings, entrance into a higher level program may be both anxiety provoking and exhilarating at the same time.

Of historical interest is one organization specifically designed to study the gifted and to aid them as necessary in social adjustment—the Clinic for the Social Adjustment of the Gifted at New York University's College of Education (Zorbaugh & Boardman, 1936). Of the 114 cases discussed as having received services at the clinic, 85 had been referred by parents and only 14 by school personnel, which was perceived by Zorbaugh and Boardman as reflecting a lack of concern on the part of the public schools with the behavior and adjustment of students. Twenty-nine of the children had IQs below the gifted "cutoff" of 130, but were siblings of gifted youngsters in treatment or were suspected of having ability greater than that shown on the Binet test. Seven of the subjects had tested at IQ 170 or higher. Of particular interest, given the year of publication, is the clinic's philosophy, cited more than once, that "when a clinic accepts a child for treatment, it frequently has to take on the whole family. The child's problems, in many cases, grow out of his family relationships, and treatment has to concern itself with parents and siblings, occasionally more intensively so than with the child originally referred as the problem" (p. 101).

Two types of service were requested for the gifted youngsters, one that could be characterized as educational advice (e.g., appropriate school) and the other as treatment for a wide variety of adjustment problems. Using a psychiatrist and a social worker, each family was studied and treatment instituted as needed. About two thirds of the children were of foreign parentage, not surprising if one considers the ferment in Europe in the mid-1930s, especially in Germany. Presumably, some of the adjustment problems could have arisen in the context of immigration.

Zorbaugh and Boardman, and obviously officials of New York University at the time, felt "no need of arguing the significance of [the clinic's] work. Gifted children are the nation's most precious resource.... These children have an enormous contribution to make—in intellectual achievement and leadership—if they can realize their possibilities" (1936, p. 108). It is interesting to note that several years later, they wrote that the "highly gifted children as a group fail to fulfill the extraordinary promise of their early years.... The resultant loss to their society will be tremendous and tragic. The problem of learning effectively to use its highly gifted citizens is a critical problem of democracy" (Zorbaugh, Boardman, & Sheldon, 1951, p. 105).

Cognitive Traits and Learning Styles

Of importance to the gifted students *and* their teachers and counselors is the knowledge that the gifted tend to have learning styles different from those of the average student. They do not necessarily all have the same exact style, but typically share many characteristics. Griggs (1991), summarizing a number of studies, asserts that gifted students are "independent (self) learners, internally controlled, persistent, perceptually strong, nonconforming, and highly motivated" (p. 67). These characteristics, or learning behaviors, may at times put the gifted in conflict with a teacher, a counselor, or their peers or parents.

Beyond the cognitive abilities that are generally the first traits noticed in identifying the gifted, these children have other characteristics that can ultimately affect their choice of companions, career, and lifestyle. For example, Baska (1989) includes among affective traits of the gifted a sense of justice, altruism, and idealism; a sense of humor; emotional intensity; perfectionism; high levels of energy; strong attachments and commitments; aesthetic sensitivity; and an early concern about death. Not all gifted youth have all of these characteristics, obviously, and among those who do share a number of them, not all use their gifts in socially constructive ways.

One behavior that can certainly be seen from different perspectives is "stick-to-itiveness," which is called "persistence" when perceived as a strength and "stubbornness" when perceived negatively. It is also called "task commitment," as gifted people tend to stay with a task until they solve the problem, create the desired product, or otherwise reach their goal. Task commitment also includes a high

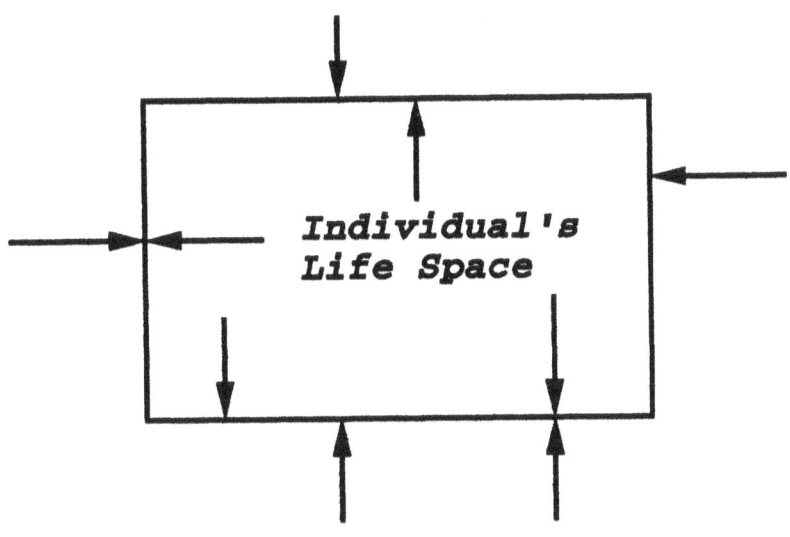

Figure 3.1. Diagrammatic View of Lewin's Field Theory

level of motivation, usually intrinsic in nature, that propels the student toward that goal. This alone suggests that teachers and counselors, working together, might need to seek alternative instructional modes for gifted students, modes that tend to exploit rather than denigrate their learning style.

Why do some individuals who appear to be gifted in their early years blossom in adolescence and early adulthood, whereas others, equally gifted in childhood, turn away from achievement? Kurt Lewin's theory provides a broad canvas on which responses to that question may be drawn. He asserted that "Behavior" is a function of the interaction of the person and his/her environment [$B = f(p,e)$] (1951, 1954). "Person" in this equation includes inherited and acquired traits of the individual, whereas "environment" includes all those forces from outside the individual, whether parental, educational, social, religious, and so forth. If the internal and external forces meet head on, there is conflict; if they do not meet head on, then the individual acts upon the environment or the environment modifies the individual in some way. Figure 3.1 demonstrates this graphically in the general sense.

28 ■ Why Give "Gifts" to Gifted?

The most common reference to the gifted is with respect to a number, the Intelligence Quotient (IQ), a score derived from performance on a standardized "intelligence" test. As has become apparent, this is not the only means of identifying gifted individuals, nor is academic ability the only realm of giftedness. Nevertheless, thinking in this narrow band for the moment, it might also be acknowledged that relatively few people ever attain their potential level of intelligence, though some come closer than others. Lewin's approach might help to explain why this difference exists.

In a series of studies, Perrone (1986) found that students, parents, and teachers agreed that six personal descriptors characterized gifted students: thought processes, task persistence, and goal orientation on the cognitive dimension and internal locus of control, social awareness, and social effectiveness on the affective dimension. Not all of these qualities, especially social awareness and social effectiveness, are apparent in younger gifted children, but thought processes advanced for the child's age often provide the first clue to potential giftedness. Task persistence (perhaps misperceived as stubbornness by unsympathetic elders) and goal orientation, sometimes termed "need to achieve," may also appear early. The other three characteristics need parental, and later, teacher guidance and encouragement to develop, as will be discussed in pages to come.

Entering School

Given the foundations for academic giftedness, what happens when the child enters school? Assume that a child speaks in sentences quite early, has an unusually large vocabulary, handles numbers at an advanced level, and has an IQ score of 158 when tested in first grade. In addition, the child asks many questions and has a high level of energy. In one family, the parents have regularly taken the child to the zoo and to "Please touch" science museums; have read to the child; have encouraged the child's curiosity; and have also taken appropriate care of the child's health, nutrition, and development in all areas. In another family, the parents have regularly "shushed" the child's questions, have not taken the child outside of the neighborhood, and have been preoccupied with their own concerns. What happens once the child enters school, as far as continued above-average cognitive performance is concerned, depends not only upon the cumulative effect of all these preschool experiences, but also on the teacher's perception of the child and subsequent actions; on peers' perceptions of the child; and on the child's interpretation of these events, perceptions, and consequent responses.

To take just two of the gifted child's characteristics that may evoke different teacher responses, consider the child's propensity toward perfectionism and a high level of energy. The perfectionism may lead to fear of making errors and thereby being perceived negatively. It may also lead to immobility or inability to make a decision, for efforts and decisions may not be the "right" ones and anxiety is again aroused. Parents and teachers alike need to emphasize to the child that to err is human, and that working *toward* excellence is more important than always being perfect.

The high level of energy may be mistakenly perceived as hyperactivity. Both parents and teachers must help the child channel this energy into productive activity, with persistence toward meaningful short- and long-term goals. "Positive use of high energy is a critical part of children's emotional development so that boredom, frustration, and a tendency toward hostile outlets for the energy do not develop" (Baska, 1989, p. 22).

If the teacher treats the child the same as all others in the class in terms of instruction or if the other children tease the child, the result is likely to present a number of areas of conflict to which the child may respond with meek acceptance, boredom, anxiety, hostility, misbehavior, or adaptation—all depending on a nonmeasurable mix of genetic makeup, temperament, experiences, reasoning ability, parental pressures, and so on. This is known in Gestalt psychology as "the whole is greater than the sum of the parts." Even identical twins in this situation have the potential to respond differently because, to however slight an extent, they have had some nonidentical experiences that can affect the "whole."

On the other hand, if the teacher recognizes that the child is unusually able and well ahead of the class in performance, if the teacher modifies assignments for the child, and if peers respond positively to the child, there are likely to be fewer areas of conflict and many more areas in which the child can continue to develop. One would expect the child to respond by maintaining a high level of performance.

Leisure, Risk Taking, and Creativity

Terman had noted that his gifted had many, varied hobbies and activities when they were children. He could report that they remained catholic in their interests in middle age. Four-fifths of them had two or more hobbies and more than a half [sic] reported having three or more. Many of them continued the activities that had interested them as children, and if they had special talents then (music or writing, for instance), they retained them in mid-life. They enjoyed membership in a variety of organizations and in service clubs. (Shurkin, 1992, p. 216)

R. M. Milgram (1991b), in her long-term studies of gifted youth, agrees that leisure activities are often critical in the development of talents as well as interests. In fact, she asserted "that leisure activities outside of school are more stable and valid indicators of giftedness than IQ scores" (p. 19). Consider, as she has, that "children who spend many hours reading, practicing an instrument, painting, or working in their 'laboratories' are developing not only intellectual abilities but also task commitment, and other cognitive and personal-social attributes that positively affect life outcomes" (p. 18).

Given that many academically gifted youngsters are described as being intellectually curious, enjoying problem solving, and welcoming unstructured situations that they can explore in their own ways, it may be appropriate to consider them as being type T personalities. In Farley's (1991) enumeration, motivating factors for type T personalities include uncertainty, novelty, much variety, complexity, ambiguity, low structure, unpredictability, high risk, and high structure. Although not all gifted youths are motivated by all of these factors, most of them, as described earlier, share many of them. As will be seen in discussing gifted students in alternative settings (see Chapter 4), these factors can be used in constructive (positive type T) or destructive (negative type T) ways. The high level of energy described by Baska (1989) can thus potentially be used to either good or harmful effect.

Within a very traditional school setting, it is these very characteristics or factors that are likely to make a teacher perceive a behavior problem rather than an agile mind. Often this is the child labeled as a "class clown." "For a child, T-mental risk taking might be taking a contrary viewpoint, for example, or questioning the teacher in the classroom" (Farley, 1991, p. 373). If, on the other hand, the teacher or another significant figure in the child's life accepts such behavior and even helps to direct it, the child may be stimulated to move forward toward creativity rather than toward socially disapproved activities such as delinquency and crime. J. G. Nelson (1992), among others, suggests the type T child or the class clown "would do better in an educational setting characterized as inductive, discovery learning, fast pace, variable pacing, discussion format, student centered, heuristic, and creative (etc.)" (p. 1248). It is no coincidence that such a setting is one that is preferred by many traditionally labeled gifted youths as well.

Gifted students are frequently placed in competitive situations. The importance and financial value of the scholarships and other awards that are given as prizes in competitions, such as the Westinghouse Talent Search or "Olympics of the Mind," certainly provide motivation to compete and win; it is not always the competition or the prize that excites gifted students. For example, Clinkenbeard (1989) found that gifted seventh and eighth graders perceived negative effects of classroom competition in self-satisfaction, continuing motivation, and related factors. These are students who frequently have the "best project" in a class, but who tend to favor projects that have high intrinsic interest even if they are more difficult than other task options. Moreover, those who favored more individualistic projects than competitive ones were particularly attuned to effort rather than simply high ability. In other words, they *enjoyed* challenge.

So Who Is the Gifted Individual?

We would have to conclude that gifted students are, or have the potential to be, adventurous, persistent, self-motivated, relatively mature, and intriguing people. They are interested in what goes on about them and tend to welcome the chance to change the world, usually for the better. They may, however, if treated inappropriately by parents or teachers, develop a fear of success (because success imperils their peer acceptance) or a fear of failure (because failure imperils their sense of self-esteem). They may be found easily—through a variety of intelligence and achievement measures—or with difficulty because of their background, state of health, or place of residence. The principal point is that they *must* be found, for their benefit and for the benefit of society.

4 The Underidentified Gifted

That gifted students come from a wide variety of socioeconomic, ethnic, and racial backgrounds is apparent when one reads about National Merit Scholars and others who win academic honors. The problem is that too often in too many school districts the culturally diverse, the handicapped, the emotionally troubled and socially maladjusted, and others who do not fit the mental image of "the gifted" are overlooked. One reason for this is that standardized intelligence tests, upon which most identification is initially based, may not be appropriate for populations of all cultures. Another reason is that some of these youngsters come from a background impoverished by language, by example, by experience, or by income. They simply have not had the same early advantages that a middle- or upper-class Caucasian child may have had.

Armour-Thomas (1992) presents a particularly coherent analysis of such factors, pointing out that in order "to make judgments about different cultural groups it is imperative that we understand the cultural influences on their performance" (p. 557). This "imperative" alerts the schools to two ideas with respect to the intellectual assessment of "different" children:

> First, our assessment procedures must be sufficiently flexible, diagnostic, and dynamic to provide not merely the presence or absence of cognitive competencies assessed at a particular point in time but must include information about the developing child's changing ecological conditions that may have enabled or impeded the manifestation of the competencies appraised. Second, intellectual assessment practices should ascertain an individual's potential for the acquisition

of the competencies of interest and to predict what interventions would most likely lead to the development and nurturance of such competencies over time. (p. 561)

The latter implication is very similar to Feuerstein's (1980) technique of evaluating and mediating children's abilities.

A third factor in the failure to identify some students who are really gifted is that society in general and bureaucracies in particular (and schools tend to be bureaucratic) often use patterns to increase efficiency and reduce costs. The difficulty is that many of the youngsters from groups to be discussed in this chapter *do not fit the pattern* and are therefore overlooked at what becomes great cost to them and to society.

B. Kerr, Colangelo, Maxey, and Christensen (1992) found that approximately 9% of the more than 55,000 high school juniors and seniors who took the ACT Assessment in spring 1988 and scored at or above the 95th percentile identified themselves as being from minority backgrounds. Asian Americans were overrepresented, with those from the poorest ethnic minority groups (blacks, Native Americans, Mexican Americans, and Hispanics) underrepresented. As these researchers pointed out, "This makes sense in light of the fact that in the United States, local socioeconomic conditions also determine the quality of education" (p. 607). Differences among the groups in desire for services from counselors are noted by these authors and offered as guidance to the schools for future action.

Economic disadvantage and parental educational disadvantage are often related and frequently are also allied to negative feelings toward the schools even in the children. The children come to the primary level ill prepared (unless they have been to an effective Head Start program), and by middle school level are sorely in need of experiences of success and peer acceptance. "If feelings of competence and acceptance are not gained in school activities, early adolescent disadvantaged students are more likely to" drop out or seek recognition for nonacademic pursuits (Braddock & McPartland, 1993, p. 155). Their capabilities—which may be considerable in one area or another—must be identified early so that they can be guided to feelings of positive self-concept before early adolescence. They will also need support from school personnel in dealing with sometimes chaotic personal lives or difficult neighborhood conditions that make long-range planning seem irrelevant.

As the number of children in our schools who come from nonmajority heritage increases, attention needs to be paid to means of assessment that are not biased against them. This has been a challenge to educators and psychologists for several years, for a long list of groups including African American, Hispanic, Chinese, Vietnamese, Native American, Filipino, Aleut, Haitian, and French Canadian. In addition to appropriate nonbiased tests, it is important to have trained bilingual examiners who are familiar with idiomatic expressions as well as the more formal language vocabulary (Schwartz, 1984). In addition, Frasier (1991) has sought to develop a profile assessment that relies on "dynamic rather than static displays of gifted behaviors" (p. 239), again recognizing that cultural differences in behavioral expectations affect children's school and test performance.

Despite the potential handicaps confronting minority students on tests, however, they can and do score well under many other circumstances. A Better Chance (ABC), a national academic talent search organization, for example, works at finding "overlooked" gifted children, especially children of color, who are about to enter high school. ABC makes it possible for these children to attend public or private secondary schools on a residential basis to prepare for college and an adult career. Those who have been part of the ABC program have compiled an outstanding college and graduate school record (Griffin, 1992), a fitting tribute to the commitment of those who work so diligently to find them.

Van Tassel-Baska (1989a), discussing the "disadvantaged gifted," has made another interesting suggestion:

> Another alternative is to state that every building in a school district will select the upper 3%, 5%, or 10% of its most talented students and then assume that the "levels of giftedness" from building to building will vary. Thus, a building that draws upon a group of economically deprived youngsters may identify a group of relatively "less gifted" (as indicated by standard test scores) youngsters than would a building that draws upon a more affluent population. (p. 57)

Early intervention—as in Head Start and Project Follow Through programs—effective teachers, and parent involvement are also critical to maximizing opportunities for the gifted disadvantaged to move toward fulfilling their potential. Administrative and community support, as well as flexibility and innovation, are necessary for these factors to be effective.

In the sections to come, the focus will be on the identification of gifted and talented students from culturally diverse (*not* culturally *deprived*), rural, handicapped, and other population groups generally not perceived as sources of gifted students. There may be fewer of them per 1,000 students than is true of those coming from more advantaged backgrounds, but they are by no means such a rarity as to be ignored, overlooked, or denied encouragement or special education appropriate to their abilities. Once identified, it is important for educators to remember, as they plan their teaching strategies, that there is considerable *within*-group heterogeneity that affects individual children's learning style, motivation, and ultimate achievement. Actually, attending to these differences may benefit all children in a school, and not just the gifted. As Kitano (1991) wrote so cogently:

> Assimilationist education for the culturally diverse gifted focuses on identifying those who score competitively with mainstream gifted students on standardized measures and providing curriculum and instruction that continue their competitiveness in mainstream society. A pluralist approach seeks to include as gifted those culturally diverse students whose high potential may be manifested in nontraditional ways. Curriculum and instruction emphasize modifying the school and classroom to accommodate diverse students' familiar learning approaches and to engage all students and teachers in democratic, cooperative interactions. Important in this view is a schooling process that empowers students to attain excellence in their own lives and to improve greater society. (pp. 15-16)

African Americans

It is highly inappropriate to group all African Americans together. In addition to variations in national heritage, some have had socioeconomic advantages that differ not at all from those of many of their Caucasian and Asian classmates whereas others have experienced economic, nutritional, and experiential deprivation. Even so, there are gifted children to be found at both extremes of the ability range and all along the continuum in between. The "trick," once past the narrow vision of some people, is to find appropriate alternative means of assessment of potential for those whose background is not that of the mythical "average American" student, that is, Eurocentric and middle class.

There is relatively little research available to suggest appropriate modes of evaluating African American students. Although some children grow up speaking primarily idiomatic English (e.g., black English), they are exposed to standard English on television as well as in school and rarely have the language limitations of many other minority groups. Nevertheless, most of the literature that is available condemns the use of traditional testing. One author offered constructive suggestions in an attempt to remedy this problem. In the view of Patton (1992), "Many young African Americans learn information better when it has human social content and is characterized by fantasy and humor. Their performance is influenced often by authorizing figures' expression of confidence or doubt, invitation or rejection" (p. 152).

This suggests for some of these youths, at least, that "a culturally sensitive, multimodal assessment and identification approach be used to identify gifted, African-American learners" (p. 153). There have been attempts to develop tests of cognitive ability more attuned to the African American experience, such as the DOVE Counter-Balance Intelligence Test (Schwartz, 1972) and the Black Intelligence Test of Cultural Homogeneity (BITCH), but they provided few clues to the ability of the individual to function effectively in school or in the larger society (Matarazzo & Pankratz, 1980).

Screening checklists should reflect behaviors valued in the community, many of which characterize gifted children from all backgrounds, such as "asks good questions," "is sensitive to others," "notices what's going on," "is a good problem solver," and so on. Patton recommends other tests as well that have been shown to be effective in identifying gifted African American youngsters, including the Kaufman Assessment Battery for Children (K-ABC) and the Torrance Tests of Creative Thinking, which are used in the broader community. The Torrance Tests and instruments similar to them, according to Renzulli (1975), "avoid the problem of evaluating the child through experiences that are common to the dominant culture, and at the same time, [help] to create a psychologically safe atmosphere which will motivate him to put forth his greatest effort" (p. 416).

It is possible that some of Patton's approach might be viewed negatively by African Americans and others—as discriminatory, demeaning, or a putdown of the child and the child's community. Care needs to be taken that the criteria selected are not so atypical that they are devalued by society and the youths themselves as encouraging "tokenism." Patton is correct, however, in recommending the use of multimodal assessment; this is the case for all students and not just African Americans.

Nomination by parents, teachers, peers, or the individual in question for inclusion in gifted programs can be, as suggested earlier, a valuable part of the process, but only if the adults have open eyes and ears and if the child perceives inclusion as worthy of attention and effort. Baldwin's (1985) Identification Matrix is one instrument that uses, in part, checklists of behaviors to help teachers and other school personnel to identify giftedness in African American children in particular and in other culturally different groups as well. The areas of giftedness described include cognitive, psychosocial, psychomotor, creative (products), task commitment (motivation), and creativity (process).

As will be discussed in Chapter 5, when gifted African American youths *are* identified, a major task may be to convince many of them that the benefits of such recognition are worth the possible loss of status with some peers and some family members.

Hispanics/Latinos

The identification of gifted youngsters from Hispanic backgrounds is complicated by the variety of environments from which their families have come—Puerto Rico, Mexico, Cuba, Argentina, Guatemala, Spain, Peru, and so on. (Note: Basques, Portuguese, and Brazilians, although technically Latinos, do not have Spanish as their basic language.) Each of these countries has its own idiomatic expressions, customs, and cultural heritages, in addition to the socioeconomic differences to be found among all groups.

Schools in the Southwestern part of the United States have traditionally dealt with Mexican American youngsters, many of them part of the migrant labor population, and more recently have enrolled children from other Central American and some South American countries. In the Southeast, especially Florida, Hispanics are more often from Cuba with some from Puerto Rico. Many Middle Atlantic cities have large Puerto Rican populations, as well as a sprinkling from other areas of Latin America. For many of the families, but by no means all of them, Spanish continues to be the language spoken at home, and for the children, at play.

A survey of experienced bilingual, English as a Second Language (ESL), and regular classroom teachers with respect to identifying gifted and talented Hispanic students revealed, to no one's real surprise, that current identification procedures are inadequate. These procedures contribute to the underrepresentation of Hispanics in programs for the gifted and overrepresentation in the ranks of those "at risk" for dropping out of school. As Bermúdez and Rakow (1990) point out, identification procedures for gifted and talented Hispanic students with limited English proficiency (LEP) "must take into account those behaviors, linguistic and cultural, that could mask giftedness. Such behaviors include non-verbal cues which often do not transfer from one cultural context to another" (p. 27).

In another study, members of the Hispanic community were asked what characteristics they perceived as important in identifying these students (Márquez, Bermúdez, & Rakow, 1992). A profile of gifted and talented Hispanic students that emerged from this study included the following characteristics:

Finds many solutions to a problem
Likes to try new things
Is good at finding other uses for things
Is interested in a variety of things
Is observant
Is creative
Is curious
Likes to read
Is motivated to learn
Asks questions (p. 123)

Note that IQ is not included. The characteristics listed reflect instead a potentially highly creative individual and certainly match well the overview of characteristics of gifted individuals discussed in Chapter 3.

The System of Multicultural Pluralistic Assessment (SOMPA) was designed by Mercer and Lewis (1979) to meet the need for a means of assessing African American and Hispanic students. Its components included the WISC-R; a parent interview; and visual, motor, and auditory tests. The parent interview was designed to elicit information about the child's health history, adaptive behavior, and sociocultural environment. An Estimated Learning Potential (ELP) score was derived, but critics questioned its ability to predict success in the majority culture.

More recently, the Screening Assessment for Gifted Elementary Students (SAGES) has been examined for use with Hispanic and Anglo youngsters (Tallent-Runnels & Martin, 1992). This test "focuses on three areas of giftedness: reasoning, school-acquired information, and divergent production" (p. 940). Although the investigators did not find that the test differentiated subjects by ethnic group membership, the test could correctly classify 93.2% of the 162 Anglo and Hispanic students.

Another use of the WISC-R, in addition to other instruments, has been in an abbreviated form that uses the Similarities and Vocabulary subtests of the Verbal scale and the Picture Arrangement and

Block Design subtests of the Performance scale as screening tools (Ortiz & Gonzalez, 1989). It was found that this abbreviated format was a valid, appropriate, and time-saving component of identification procedures with Hispanic students.

R. Strom, Johnson, S. Strom, and P. Strom (1992) used less traditional methods to identify potentially gifted 4- to 8-year-olds who, with some parent involvement, would attend a summer institute in Arizona. In addition to the DIAL-R screening instrument that identifies children at either extreme of school readiness, teacher nomination and creativity scores (Torrance Tests of Creative Thinking, Figural subtest B) were used to select the institute participants. Selection by these means was supported generally by the children's scores on subtests of the Structure of Intellect (SOI) Tests. In addition, parents were asked to complete the Parent as a Teacher Inventory, in English or Spanish, to provide clues to parenting in the areas of creativity, frustration, control, play, and teaching learning (or the parent's self-concept of his/her ability to encourage intellectual development in the children). This was preparatory to four parent sessions that explained the scores, answered parental questions, and sought to keep the parents involved in their children's education.

In the Miami area, M. S. Scott, Perou, Urbano, Hogan, and Gold (1992) sought to discover the role of white, Hispanic, and black parents in the placement of their children in the gifted program (Grades 3-5) and in their awareness of their children's giftedness. Questions in the latter area sought to elicit the parents' perceptions of the child as unusually observant, as exceptional in learning or memory, as having superior skills in knowledge or communication skills, as a leader, or as strongly motivated to learn. All of the children had been identified through an individual intelligence test, such as the WISC-R. Mothers in all three groups cited five attributes suggesting giftedness: (early) reading, memory, above peers (in ability), talking early, and learning quickly. Only the Hispanic mothers also listed communication/expressive skills, observant, and excelling in school (p. 135). The Hispanic and black parents, however, were less likely to request the evaluation of their children necessary for special placement than was true of white parents.

M. S. Scott et al. suggested on the basis of this study that "the identification of minority students might be enhanced through a public education program which alerted parents to those characteristics which might indicate giftedness and which informed them about the availability and function of educational programs for gifted students" (p. 139).

This idea seems worth pursuing in other venues as well. It might also be important to build parent-school bridges even prior to such a campaign so that the Spanish-speaking parents, particularly, feel more comfortable even approaching a teacher or counselor to make requests for information. Both the Strom and Scott studies, as well as others, stress the importance of involving parents early, but also emphasize the reticence of these parents to seek out educators in an effort to help their children. The presence of more teachers and other staff members who are effectively bilingual, or at least able to speak some Spanish, might reduce some of that reticence.

Asians and Pacific Islanders

Educators accustomed to dealing with highly motivated, high-achieving Asian students have in the past 20 years or so had to accommodate to a greater variety of youths from the Far East. The historical and cultural differences between earlier Asian immigrants and more recent arrivals reflect not only a broader national base but also marked socioeconomic differences. This can be exemplified by looking at the Vietnamese who arrived in the early 1970s and those who have arrived more recently. "The earlier Vietnamese, on the whole, were well educated, spoke English, and were from the middle class. They had the skills to propel themselves upward on the U.S. social and economic ladder" (R. Woliver & G. M. Woliver, 1991, p. 248). Some later émigrés did not possess such skills and therefore had more difficulty adjusting to U.S. life. Other more recent immigrants have frequently come from rural areas of Vietnam, Korea, Laos, India, Pakistan, and other countries, where they did not have the same opportunities as more affluent urban residents. In addition, many of them barely escaped with their lives from war-torn countries where whatever innate giftedness they may have had was employed in survival strategies.

Traditionally, education, achievement, and the work ethic were highly valued in the immigrant Chinese and Japanese communities. Parents often directed their children (mainly their sons in earlier generations) toward mathematics and the sciences, where they would be less likely to experience racism or interpersonal hostility (Isser & Schwartz, 1985). Many Asians and Hawaiians tend to value obedience, indirect communication, and group orientation above individualism, perfectionism, and reticence, all of which contribute to their *under*identification as gifted in the classroom unless they score well on standardized intelligence tests. Flynn (1991) argues that these environmental factors, rather than genetic ones, are primarily responsible for the "overachievement" of Asian students. As he concludes, "There is an irony in the fact that they overcame bias wherever they encountered it and yet, never excelled on the putatively unbiased IQ test" (p. 141).

Teachers are often viewed by Asians as authority figures and accorded great respect, so that traditionally a teacher's statement would never be disputed. "In the view of both Asians and Hawaiians, questions are seen as a challenge, not as an invitation to dialogue; thus, students are afraid to risk giving the 'wrong' answer and feeling humiliated. They prefer to withdraw from such challenges" (R. Woliver & G. M. Woliver, 1991, p. 252).

With many Asian American students, we see the role of the fear of failure in operation rather than the fear of success. Traditionally, peoples of the Eastern Hemisphere have placed great importance on not shaming the family, but rather bringing quiet praise to the family name. The fear of failure reflects this perspective.

Native Americans

The negative stereotypes attached to Native Americans as "children of nature" and savages in the five centuries since Europeans "discovered" America persist even today. Feagin (1989) gives a number of examples of these stereotypes still to be found in textbooks at all levels as well as in social distance studies. Tribes are not differentiated in ethos or mores, and the attitudes that result affect many interracial activities. For example, the Harvard University *Encyclopedia of American Ethnic Groups* (1975), combined "the more than 170 Native American groups into one very large group" (Garcia, 1991, p. 79). They are given a little more than half a page more in this text in a discussion of "stereotyping and self-fulfilling prophecy" (p. 115). In fact, in searching for information on the gifted among Native American populations, it was almost impossible to find references either to a tribal or the larger group even in texts on multiculturalism!

"Between 1950 and 1980 the number of Native American children attending school has increased by one million, yet research about these Americans has actually declined in the last quarter century" (Kierstead & Wagner, 1993, p. 93). The one concrete reference to Native Americans in a major edited work on the gifted and talented is to legislation passed in the 98th Congress and proposed in the 99th Congress that *might* benefit gifted and talented Native Americans (DeLeon & VandenBos, 1985, p. 420).

One of the difficulties in identifying gifted students among Native Americans is that their cultural heritage often emphasizes cooperation rather than competition, the opposite of what most U.S. schools stress. In addition, although these children are taught to do their best, that is, to compete with themselves, they are also taught not to stand out from others. In practice, this means that the Native American child whose tribe teaches these values will not respond in class if he or she knows that there are classmates who do not know the correct answer. Dakota Indians also taught that it was wrong to answer a question unless the respondent was certain that the answer was correct.

> The effect this would have upon intelligence tests, in which the subject is advised to "guess" when not sure and is urged to "try his best" on a difficult problem, can be readily foreseen. The child who refuses to give any answer unless he is certain of its correctness will lose many points that he might have earned through partial credits and chance successes. (Anastasi & Foley, 1958, p. 331)

Strictly speaking, it is difficult to define giftedness from the Navajo point of view, according to Abbott (1982), and according to a chart, "The Ontogeny of Navajo thought development," she includes (p. 12), it would be adolescence before a child even begins to think for himself or herself. Giftedness, in the Navajo sense, focuses on traditional lifestyle and activities (or the integration of these with the ways of the dominant culture) and on listening, thinking with a purpose, and task commitment. Similarly, if examined closely, the abilities valued in other tribal groups may well depend upon the tribe's lifestyle. For example, in looking at cultural variations from the Arctic to the Mexican border, McShane and Berry (1988) noted the importance to hunter-gatherer tribes (such as the Inuit of Alaska and Canada) of visual, spatial, and practical abilities. Verbal skills would have a lower priority, so consequently would not be stressed as an area in which to excel among those groups. Verbal skills would also be affected by sociocultural influences on linguistics, perhaps dictating precise ways of asking or responding to questions or to whom to speak and under what circumstances.

McShane and Plas (1984), in their review of 35 studies that examined the performance of Native Americans from a variety of tribes on the Wechsler Intelligence Scales (Wechsler Preschool and Primary Scale of Intelligence/WPPSI, Wechsler Intelligence Scale for Children/WISC, and Wechsler Adult Intelligence Scale/WAIS), cited other factors that appeared to affect achievement levels on the tests. These included fetal alcohol syndrome, otitis media, lead poisoning, problems related to left-right hemispheric lateralization, and an emphasis on nonverbal communication. Naglieri (1984), who used both the WISC-R and the Kaufman Assessment Battery for Children (K-ABC) with his 35 Navajo child subjects found that the two measures

> may not yield equal estimates of intellectual functioning for Navajo children. Because these children score lower on the Verbal than on the Performance scale and earn their lowest WISC-R subtest score on Vocabulary and their lowest K-ABC subtest scores on tests that require verbalizations, a logical explanation for the K-ABC/WISC-R discrepancy may be the influence of the English language on the Wechsler scale. (pp. 376-377)

Because the K-ABC can be administered in Navajo, unlike the Wechsler scales, it may provide the more valid picture of cognitive intelligence.

Although the foregoing studies report efforts to locate a valid means of evaluating the intellectual functioning of Native American students, Davidson (1992) tried to compare Native American and white subjects who were already identified as having above-average or superior intellectual abilities. She found that the two groups did not differ significantly in the assessment of overall or general intelligence on the K-ABC Mental Processing Composite, but each group outperformed the other on different subtests. Analysis of the abilities demonstrated on these subtests lends credence, in Davidson's comments, "to the view that American Indian subjects exhibited their greatest strengths in those sub-tests which required simultaneous processing—without interference from a requirement for secondary processing of a very different type—in combination with spatial/abilities ability" (p. 114). As she suggests, this information should guide teachers in the methods of instruction they use with Native American students, in choice of areas in which there should be remedial instruction, and in recognition of individual differences *within* cultural groups.

Summaries of other studies that used either the Wechsler scales or the K-ABC with Sioux, Ojibwa, and Navajo children indicate that these youngsters tend to obtain higher scores on performance scales than on verbal scales (Cummings & Merrell, 1993). This would tend to depress the number identified as gifted students even if the cultural and socioeconomic factors were absent. Other factors to be considered in working with Native American children are their living conditions (usually rural and relatively poor; possibly isolated), school attendance (often low), and English-language competence (variable). Low English-language competence may be due to lack of fluency in English or to a general language dysfunction that is the result of repeated (and largely untreated) episodes of otitis media, as noted earlier. In any case, it is imperative that more attention be paid to the effect of varied tribal teachings as well as the physical conditions of Native American children's lives if the gifted among them are to be located.

Rural Students

Basic education is still dominated by the calendar that befitted an agricultural nation, but its tests and texts no longer ask questions or use illustrations related to the farm or to isolated communities. Indeed, students in rural areas, especially those from poverty backgrounds, are often disadvantaged by procedures now used to identify gifted students. As Spicker (1992) pointed out, "Such children often have had limited urban travel experiences; have been exposed to few educational toys, books, magazines, and school-related materials in the home; and are likely to come from families whose adult members have a minimal formal education" (p. 62). In this, they may be little different from urban economically disadvantaged youngsters, even relative to the urban travel experiences factor.

Spicker worked with teachers of these children, many of whom were descended from families from Appalachia, pointing out atypical behaviors that might indicate giftedness among their elementary students. These included creativity, ability to sequence events, exceptional ability in one area and weakness in others, and higher nonverbal than verbal performance. In addition, parents were asked about their children's "ability or interest in fixing things, making things, collecting things, writing things, and reading things" (p. 63). Their responses often identified a child with unusual capabilities in nonacademic endeavors. A Pioneer Contest for fourth graders, with performance criteria of creativity, critical thinking, logic, and reasoning ability, was used as an additional means of identifying gifted children. The need for multifaceted assessment is as evident for these youngsters as for those from other countries or cultures.

Again it becomes apparent that parents are a valuable source for identifying gifted youngsters. Gaining their support for a higher powered education for their children may be problematic in some cases, however, if the parents perceive this as potentially causing loss of their children in adulthood as co-workers on the farm or as support in the parents' later years.

Physically or Otherwise Handicapped

Ludwig van Beethoven, Itzhak Perlman, and Ray Charles are three names well known to music lovers. Each man is, or was, a gifted musician who also was handicapped. Beethoven composed some of his finest music after he became severely hearing impaired; Perlman thrills listeners with his violin virtuosity though he sits rather than stands as a soloist because of his orthopedic handicap; and Charles plays the piano with talent and zest though his blindness prevents him from reading a note. Similarly, Albert Einstein and Winston Churchill were regarded as poor students, possibly with what we would today call learning disabilities, yet their adult accomplishments certainly indicate that they were highly gifted in cognitive areas. Despite these well-known examples, too often the presence of a sensory or other physical disability blinds adults to heightened abilities that a child may have.

The learning disabled, for example, by definition have average or better intelligence with a specific learning problem. That problem may obscure giftedness in another area. Many of these children may have an attention deficit disorder or hyperactivity in addition to the specific problem that results in incomplete assignments or behavior problems. Boodoo, Bradley, Frontera, Pitts, and Wright (1989) present the different conflicting characteristics that may keep a gifted learning-disabled (GLD) child from being appropriately identified and educated. As they point out, "All that is known for certain is that GLD children possess two general traits: They have both extraordinary strengths and severe weaknesses. Additionally, this paradox may lead to poor self-concept which may manifest itself in behavior problems" (p. 111).

Hearing and visual impairments or other physical disabilities may also provide an obstacle to determining a child's assets, as adults may tend to focus exclusively on the handicapping condition. Such a focus can contribute to the child developing an external locus of control, becoming field dependent, and displaying learned helplessness. In addition, the physical problems often have a genetic component that may be related to neurological impairment, thereby interfering with academic performance to some extent (Bireley, 1991). If, to further confound the odds, the student comes from a lower- or middle-class socioeconomic background, there is even less likelihood that giftedness will be perceived (Minner, 1990).

Each school district is required to have a "child-find" program to screen all children for handicapping conditions as they enter school in kindergarten or through transfer. The child-find mechanism is also a good way to search for gifted handicapped children. Early identification is crucial so that intervention can begin. (Seeley, 1989b, p. 34)

As Torrance (1984) has indicated, where such handicaps exist, procedures for identifying gifts and talents must "permit responses in a modality possible for the student" (p. 155). One of the possibilities raised by Whitmore (1985) is to compare the performance of children with similar handicaps. She also suggests as evidence of giftedness, particularly where the ability to use oral language is absent, the presence (and demonstration) of unusual memory for facts and events, exceptional interest and drive, an apparent high level of comprehension, and unusual problem-solving techniques.

The intervention that ensues should include an alliance between the special education personnel and the teacher of the gifted to ensure that implementation of the child's IEP stresses the use of the child's abilities to compensate for weaknesses and develop strategies to cope with school tasks. Use of new technological aids to enhance communication will also aid the gifted handicapped child to participate in mainstream and special programs.

Students in Alternative Settings

In some communities, alternative schools have been provided, usually at the secondary level, for students unable or unwilling to function in the regular schools. Depending upon the size of the school, the staff-student ratio, and the philosophy of the program, the students may simply mark time until they reach school-leaving age or may be stimulated to change their motivation, attitudes, and school (if not test) performance. Some of the students are emotionally troubled or "disaffected"; others may be regarded as delinquents. Because they tend to score poorly on tests and are often perceived negatively by school district personnel, they are rarely considered as possibly gifted or talented. They would have to be classified as "gifted underachievers" even though they may never have obtained a test score identifying them as gifted. (Note that this situation is somewhat different from that of the child who scores well on intelligence tests but is labeled an "underachiever" by the well-meaning counselor if class grades are not quite as high as might be expected.)

General perceptions may be in error. A study of middle school students perceived as nonachievers or troublemakers, but identified as "potentially able" showed that they earned higher grades and had fewer disciplinary problems in school after participating in a summer program for gifted and talented students (Schwartz & Fischman, 1984). In a study focused specifically on an alternative-learning school population, Osborne and Byrnes (1990) used nontraditional as well as traditional means of identifying potentially gifted students:

> The criteria for exceptionality in this study were: scores in the top 5% on the standardized tests used for identification; and/or nominations by two or more teachers; and/or the top 5% of students nominated by peers. Students were defined as potentially gifted and talented if they possessed any *one* or several of a broad range of exceptional abilities based on the above definition [an earlier version of the one cited on p. 9] and criteria. (p. 144)

Of 100 students enrolled in the 11th and 12th grades at the center, data were collected on 93, and 8 (8%) of these were identified as potentially gifted and talented. None of them met the standardized test criterion, but these seven males and one female qualified by their scores on a biographical inventory that measured creative ability and attitudes and participation in leadership activities ($n = 3$), and/or teacher-nomination by two or more teachers ($n = 5$), and/or peer-nomination by peers ($n = 4$). "Further support of their potential giftedness was validated through classroom observations and interviews. The identified students were the ones to draw, write poetry and stories, work on the school paper, and participate in their own musical groups. They provided leadership in the classroom and organized out-of-school activities" (p. 145).

Whether the identification led these youths to college or to unanticipated careers is not yet known. However, one might expect that teachers would have changed their interpretation of some behaviors as a result of these identifications.

In studying an identified juvenile delinquent population ($N = 288$), Harvey and Seeley (1984) used a Wechsler Scale, the Torrance Tests of Creative Thinking, and the Wide Range Achievement Test (WRAT). The full assessment was completed by 114 subjects and included questionnaires and data on each youth's family and school background. From this group, 48 were found to be gifted in some way, with 40 scoring in the top 3% on the measures. The gifted students were characterized by high performance scores on the Wechsler Scale and high levels of fluid intelligence, general fluency, and general intelligence on the other measures. The findings suggested "that these delinquent subjects used their creative and intellectual abilities differently and in opposite ways to achieve their basic school skills. . . . Once in the classroom, those students who used their creative ability achieved less well than those who used their intellectual skills" (p. 77). They were also characterized by a high level of creative energy that was related to both intellectual and divergent thinking abilities. As these capacities are often not valued in the classroom, these students usually do not attain high grades and are rarely recognized for their positive qualities.

Similarly, a British study of gifted delinquents (Brooks, 1980) found that compared with a control group of less gifted peers, the gifted delinquents were much more likely to be educational underachievers. Brooks cites a number of tendencies in members of the gifted group that, "under certain circumstances, particularly predispose them to some degree of emotional or developmental disturbance resulting in delinquent behavior" (pp. 216-217). These include:

1. A "heightened sensitivity" to experience
2. A "potentially heightened level of intellectual curiosity which, unless satisfied, may lead to feelings of frustration, anxiety, or even rejection"
3. Potentially higher levels of creativity and perception, though the latter may sometimes be unrealistic
4. Heightened critical faculties that make them skeptical of social dogmas
5. A stronger sense of self-regard that may make them seem to be "insufferably arrogant"
6. Stronger, often hostile, reactions to changes in environment
7. Potential leadership ability, possibly related to their self-regard (pp. 216-217)

These tendencies are even more detailed than those offered by Harvey and Seeley (1984) and are often equally devalued by schools. The probability of these tendencies leading to achievement in delinquent behaviors rather than academic pursuits is exacerbated, according to Brooks, by "interrupted" father-child relationships, inability of the family to deal with the child's special talents, isolation from peers, resentment of adults, and frustration of potential.

In a later study of 128 high-ability at-risk high school students, Seeley (1989b) found that factors contributing to underachievement included:

1. Being middle or youngest in the family (90%)

2. Frequency of school change
3. Teacher indifference
4. Family disruption
5. Discriminatory handling by the school of behavior conflicts among minority students as compared with majority students with the same conflicts (p. 32)

Obviously, schools cannot control a student's standing in the family or disruption in the family (although counseling could be provided to reduce its impact); they cannot even always control the frequency of school change. This constellation of tendencies and environmental factors that place the youth at risk, however, should be a warning for early identification and preventive action by school personnel. Beneficial outcomes depend upon teachers and counselors being made aware of the ways in which these tendencies and factors can interact. Teacher indifference can be overcome and discrimination avoided with in-service courses for teachers and administrators alike. Early intervention programs, especially at the preschool level, can help to build the child's self-esteem, a necessary ingredient for prevention of later problems that may necessitate remediation.

Gifted Underachievers

As we have already seen, youngsters from a variety of special populations are frequently not identified as being gifted or talented. There are also young students who are gifted, but who perform at levels below their abilities because of a variety of social or emotional factors. "Underachievement is a pervasive problem which results in a tremendous waste of human potential in this country, even among our most able students" (Schneider, 1991).

Why should children, especially those who are gifted, *under-achieve*? In Whitmore's (1988) view, "gifted children who are significantly different from their peers not only in cognitive capabilities but also in personality characteristics, and are in an educational setting that is academically unchallenging, socially unrewarding, and generally stifling to the expression and development of their giftedness, are acutely at risk" (p. 11). Underachievement then leads to lowered self-esteem, lack of self-satisfaction, and further underachievement in a vicious cycle.

Underachievement may also be a passive-aggressive response to parents who are overdemanding or place too much responsibility on their gifted child at too early an age, or it may be a manipulative technique used by the child to gain concessions from the parents (Rimm & Lowe, 1988). Other factors in the family environment that can contribute to underachievement by gifted youth are itemized by Rimm and Lowe, and include some of the factors to be discussed below.

One of the saddest examples of "what might have been" is 12-year-old Crystal. According to her mother, "Crystal was once slated for a kindergarten for gifted students, 'but she would have had to take a bus.'" Today, as a seventh grader with what her teachers call "an attitude," Crystal is assigned to a resource room designed to give troubled students individual attention. "Crystal slumped on her desk. 'We just sit there,' she said later. 'They are supposed to help you with stuff you don't understand. But I understand everything so I just sit there'" (Manegold, 1993, p. B7). This possibly gifted underachiever could easily fit into the group of students in "alternative settings" discussed earlier. There, at least, she might be properly identified and possibly helped.

There are obvious difficulties in identifying the underachieving gifted student, not the least of which is the complexity of the teacher's day and duties. However, Whitmore (1985) asserts that "if a teacher genuinely invites communication from the child, and listens carefully, giftedness can often be detected in under-achievers.... Second, involve the child in problem-solving tasks requiring higher levels of thinking" (p. 105). Whitmore believes that the first step can reveal advanced language, ideas, and extracurricular activities, whereas the second step may suggest unusual creativity or self-directed learning. She does point out, however, that these "characteristics are most easily identified in young children before self-expression becomes repressed and attitudes influencing behaviour are firmly set" (p. 105).

Perhaps the most obvious factor in underachievement is negative self-esteem, the perception that "I *can't*." Indeed, one of the characteristics of gifted underachievers appears to be poor coping skills (Gallagher, 1991). It is interesting that Terman and his associates had much earlier found that this weakness apparent in the school records of gifted underachieving males (Terman & Oden, 1947). They also found that these individuals, as compared with their achieving peers, lacked self-confidence, did not persevere at tasks as well, and had feelings of inferiority. In most cases, these traits are remediable if treated appropriately.

Inappropriate or inadequate cognitive processing skills may also contribute to underachievement. For example, Redding (1990) found that underachieving gifted adolescents, as compared with their achieving peers, needed to be taught skills that would aid them in successfully completing tasks that required "rote learning, detail-analysis, and convergent problem solving"—in other words, better study habits and somewhat altered learning styles (p. 74). These strategies, which tend to be less popular than divergent thinking skills with gifted students, are necessary at times within most school systems and should be dealt with as motivational rather than ability factors.

There may also be an undiagnosed learning deficit or other organic disorder that inhibits achievement. In other cases, barriers have been established in the environment that inhibit the child's explorations or expansions of effort. The first task, obviously, is to identify these children; the second, to provide necessary changes so that they *can* flourish (Supplee, 1990).

There is, as part of the self-perception aspect, the question of attributions of success and failure. Does the gifted child have an internal or external locus of control? In one study comparing gifted underachievers, gifted achievers, and nongifted elementary level students, Laffoon, Jenkins-Friedman, and Tollefson (1989) found that the gifted underachievers, more than students in either of the other groups, attributed their successes to their abilities and their failures to luck or fate. It is suggested that these youngsters be taught the role of effort as opposed to luck in an attempt to help them develop a more realistic perspective and enhance their performance.

Another factor in underachievement, especially as bright youngsters move into early adolescence, is a belief that a person is born with a fixed amount of intelligence. Accordingly, they seek to perform well on tasks so as to confirm their abilities, but tend to avoid new challenges that might reveal their limitations ("When bright kids," 1992). This pattern seems to occur more often with girls than with boys. It is related to a fear of failure, the admission that one is not perfect, as well as to an external locus of control.

Gallagher separates environmental factors from personal or family factors (1991). Peer groups, especially those in underprivileged neighborhoods or with a delinquent bent, are among the antiacademic environmental factors, though if the individual's ability is used in the interests of the group's activities it might be regarded less negatively. Race, in the context of "political correctness," also plays a role in underachievement. According to Ford (1993), the gifted black student who is positively oriented toward academic achievement may well be perceived by peers as "acting white," a definite "no-no" in some areas. Ford found further that although "Black students support the American achievement ideology and also consider school to be important or very important, . . . they do not necessarily put forth the effort required to achieve at their optimal level—as indicated by their self-reports and teacher feedback of low effort" (p. 295). There also appeared to be a somewhat greater emphasis on luck than effort among the subjects. Ford, like Laffoon et al. (1989), therefore stresses the need for educators to help black students perceive a positive relationship between effort and success.

Another negative environmental influence is the antielitist attitude found in many communities (see pp. 63-66 for a discussion of this factor). Whether the root of such an attitude is simple jealousy or resentment, or something else, it is conveyed to the children who consequently hide whatever talents they may have. This results in yet another instance of underachievement.

Conclusion

The underidentified gifted are clearly among the underserved in our schools. If underserved, they may decide to become underschooled as well, that is, school dropouts in body or in spirit. Because many of the underidentified gifted are members of groups already considered socioeconomically disadvantaged, being underserved adds insult to injury, as it were, and increases the probability that these individuals will become dependents of society rather than contributors to it.

5 Fostering Giftedness

In sharp contrast to the belief of those who allege that the gifted will make it on their own is the reality that for most gifted youth, there is a need for someone to nurture the gifts, to open the doors of opportunity, to support the nascent efforts, and generally to enable the gifted to develop their abilities and use them in constructive ways. Parents and other early caretakers are usually the first to notice a child's unusual behaviors. The child may be the next one to realize that he or she does things differently than friends or siblings, with the reactions of those peers becoming more and more important to the child as he/she moves on to school and to adolescence. Classroom teachers and, where available, school counselors determine to a great extent whether education plays a constructive or deleterious role in the gifted child's development. Additionally, these individuals are subject to some extent to peer and community attitudes toward difference, specifically in this case giftedness.

If our commitment is to foster giftedness, then we must understand the role that each of these people or groups plays in the life of the gifted child. It is also important to be aware of the ways in which these roles can be misplayed.

Parental Role

One can certainly attribute part of a gifted individual's talents to the genetic potential transmitted from parents to child. However, it is difficult for that potential to develop if the environment is unstimulating, or even punitive, although some invulnerable children do overcome their negative beginnings (Brown & Rhodes, 1991).

Apart from nurturing the physical and emotional health of children, it is important that parents supply the foundations for other characteristics found among the gifted, such as answering questions, modeling task commitment, or directing children to resources that might provide enlightenment.

It is equally important that parents try to avoid demanding perfect performance by the gifted child at all times at any age, for "inability to meet the perceived expectations is most distressing" (Perez, 1980, p. 11). Indeed, as already noted, the inability to meet one's own or others' demands for perfection may lead the gifted child to become a gifted underachiever. Combined with high levels of pressure for achievement there may be unreasonable expectations for behavior that are more in keeping with the child's mental age than his/her chronological age. If parents "tend to view the gifted child as immature or undisciplined when age-typical behaviors occur (e.g., tears of frustration, forgetfulness, silliness) . . . [they] may admonish or punish the child for behavior that is accepted in age-mates" (Whitmore, 1988, p. 12). All of these situations are unfair to the child.

M. Scott (1988) identified four "key attitudinal and behavioral differences [that] appear to be consistently found in families of successful G/T/C children" (p. 8). These include:

1. Genuine interest in, respect for, and noncontingent acceptance of the child
2. Ongoing communication and involvement with the child, with an emphasis on actively spending time with the child
3. Conveying an attitude of persistence
4. Allowing the child freedom or independence to explore, to take risks, and to think for him/herself

Clearly, these are attitudes and behaviors that would benefit virtually all children, but they appear to be critical for gifted, talented, and creative children. One cannot say that these factors are essential, however, for gifted children have succeeded without such parental behaviors, though they might have reached even greater goals had they had the appropriate support.

In the case of economically disadvantaged gifted adolescents, Van Tassel-Baska (1989b) found that the role of one or both parents, and sometimes a grandmother or other figure in the extended family, was critical. When family members valued education highly, the student's achievement motivation appeared to be stimulated. The parents or grandmother sought out programs that would provide opportunities for the gifted child. If the family does not supply this backing or support, there is the risk that the achievement will diminish, unless, of course, the child is fortunate enough to be identified by a teacher or other figure who can act as mentor.

Of particular concern are Hispanic females, who have been described as "the most at risk of all students" (Tinajero, 1992, p. 28). They often come from poor homes where there are few models for finishing high school or for excelling. Mothers, traditionally strong influences on their children, have had little positive experience with education. One program that has sought to use maternal influence in a motivating way is a mother-daughter program at the University of Texas at El Paso directed toward sixth-grade girls. It is mentioned here because mother and daughter participation in the program has apparently identified academically able girls, encouraged them to take advanced level and honors courses en route to college, and raised the consciousness of the mothers to the point that the mothers have become a significant motivating force for continuing education (Tinajero, 1992).

An important task for parents is to consider the impact of the gifted label on their talented child (and on their other children) and act thoughtfully afterward. In the mid-1930s during the heyday of child stars like Shirley Temple, much was written about manipulative mothers, with most of the reaction to them being negative. The musical *Gypsy* portrays such a woman in the extreme. Similarly, questions are raised about the parental role in the training of the athletically talented in tennis, ice skating, and gymnastics. Do the parents push the child to practice (or study) so hard in the effort to win a blue ribbon (or coveted prize) that the child has no room in the day for normal peer activities or simply for privacy and relaxation? How do the parents feel about having a child labeled gifted?

These questions become even more critical for families where there is a profoundly gifted child (IQ 170+). Parents may be overwhelmed by the news or by witnessing the child's extraordinary abilities. They certainly have the responsibility to become well informed about educational options, which may include home schooling, private school, radical acceleration, or another avenue, so that they can discuss these appropriately with school authorities and can themselves make decisions for their children. The financial stress upon the family to provide needed resources may be considerable, and the emotional demands on the parents from an early age may also be great (Silverman & Kearney, 1989). Unfortunately, even with an unusually gifted child, some parents may not assume their appropriate role, either because of their own inadequacies as adults or because of hostility, resentment, or other negative attitudes.

Even closer to home, when there are other children in the family, what is the effect of the gifted or talented label on sibling relationships? In a study of 144 families whose first- or secondborn child was attending an enrichment program for gifted middle and secondary school children at the University of Virginia, Tuttle and Cornell (1993) surveyed the parents, siblings, and students to try to answer this question. Emphasis was placed on the maternal use of a gifted label with respect to her child(ren). The major finding of the study was "that labeling was associated with a more positive report of the sibling relationship when firstborns were labeled, but a less positive report of the relationship when secondborns were labeled" (p. 408). This may be, as the authors indicate, because there is a common expectation that firstborns are more achievement oriented than later born children. Parental partiality was not a statistically significant factor in the relationship. However, parents of gifted children are advised to encourage all their children to "excel in the areas that are most congruent with their natural abilities and interests" (p. 409). Indeed, this is a wise guideline for all parents, whether their children are gifted or not.

Studies in this area reviewed by Keirouz (1990) yield conflicting conclusions. Siblings' reactions can depend upon whether their own performance is being compared in the same arena with that of the gifted child, or in different arenas; on how close the siblings are in age; and on how involved the parents are with the gifted child as compared with the less gifted sibling(s). Clearly, it is difficult to generalize when each constellation of factors is unique.

Families of gifted children can have problems that bring them to psychotherapists for help. In some cases, the children manipulate their parents by a misuse of their intelligence and the parents simply refuse to confront this pattern or their own immobility until a crisis arises (Wendorf & Frey, 1985). Those parents who are less well endowed intellectually than their gifted child(ren) may be intimidated by the offspring. Sometimes, one parent perceives the child as gifted and the other does not, precipitating a marital crisis (Keirouz, 1990). Other presenting concerns involve a nongifted child (perhaps even academically handicapped) in the family, emotional immaturity in the gifted, or passive-aggressive underachievement by the gifted child. Wendorf and Frey (1985) make the point that the therapist must determine whether the presenting problem is primarily one involving a dysfunctional family or one deriving from a home-school conflict, and then work out the appropriate therapeutic format.

In an era of relatively high divorce rates resulting in many single-parent families and second- or subsequent-marriage families, one must also consider the impact of separation and divorce on the performance of gifted children. Certainly the effects differ by age, acrimony of the divorce in both its initial and later stages, and the child's inner resources (Kaslow & Schwartz, 1987; T. E. Smith, 1992). Relatively little research has been done in this area, however, with specific regard to gifted children. If their lives are being complicated by parental divorce (and possibly remarriage), and especially if they are being buffeted by continuing conflict between the adults, it might be expected that their response could vary from underachievement (perhaps as a way of gaining attention from their parents) to total involvement in academic and personal pursuits as a means of shutting out these unpleasant events. In either case, these youngsters, as well as nongifted peers in the same situation, will generally profit from support groups and supportive school personnel. Attention must also be drawn to stereotypical negative teacher expectations with regard to children of divorce, as they may cloud perceptions of giftedness (J. A. Rogers & Nielson, 1993).

From another point of view, that of the schools, parents are often the first to recognize their children's gifts and can certainly identify their talents and unique behaviors on parent nomination forms. Additionally, the schools should involve the parents in planning and implementing programs not only for their own children, but for all of the gifted youngsters. Workshops for parents to help them to know how to deal with the gifted child in the larger context of the family, learning from each other as well as from school personnel, can reduce familial tensions. Children, parents, and schools will all benefit from such consultation and cooperation.

Regrettably, where the school district fails to provide adequate and appropriate educational opportunities for gifted children, their parents may have to become forceful advocates. About half of the states mandate special education services for gifted children to parallel those provided to handicapped children, but it may be necessary to take a district through due process hearings and to court to obtain the most appropriate instruction for a child within the "district's existing, regular, and special education curricular offerings" (Karnes & Marquardt, 1988, p. 361).

Apart from providing a supportive environment, it is helpful to gifted children if their parents are aware of opportunities that will help to maintain, sharpen, or advance the children's abilities and then encourage the children to participate. Several higher education institutions sponsor such programs specifically for minority or otherwise disadvantaged but potentially gifted students (e.g., the University of Texas at El Paso program discussed above). One such program, the Skills Reinforcement Project developed by the Johns Hopkins University Center for Talented Youth, focused on sixth-grade minority and disadvantaged children, providing weekend classes and a 2-week residential summer program. Slightly older academically talented minority youth attended the same college program, and minority college students participated as tutors (Lynch & Mills, 1993).

Whether the parents take the trouble to find these programs and to help their gifted children participate in them becomes the critical factor to the children. The parental action is a sign that the child and his/her ability or talent is valued by the parent(s), and this positive attitude is itself a stimulant to the child to move forward and to try to go further.

The Role of Peers

As has already been noted in discussing the underidentified gifted, in many settings gifted youngsters must make great efforts to hide their abilities from peers if they are to maintain acceptance by them. Similarly, as will be seen in discussing gifted girls, many of them learn very early to hide their competence in order to be accepted by classmates, or in adolescence, to be viewed positively by potential dates. Obviously these situations detract from the gifted child's performance and may contribute instead to underachievement. Because this is undesirable from the point of view of enabling the gifted to achieve and ultimately to contribute to society, in what ways might interaction with peers be turned to fostering giftedness?

One way to reduce isolation for the gifted is to have more than one gifted student in a class, and perhaps even to be certain that each of the gifted students is made aware of the others' abilities so that they can seek common ground on which to build a relationship. If this is a mainstreamed class rather than a tracked one, the gifted may be encouraged, from time to time, to embark on a challenging project of mutual interest and benefit to them and their classmates.

Second, as Whitmore (1988) correctly points out, "The teacher must set standards for student conduct that do not permit ridicule or exclusion of individuals and use class meetings and conflict resolution techniques to solve social problems in the classroom" (p. 13). This may be more difficult in some school settings than others, but it is a policy that needs to be in force in each classroom from the opening day of the school year. Further, the teacher must model the desired appropriate behavior if the gifted students' peers are to learn it.

Being different from one's peers by virtue of race, religion, handicap, talent, or any other characteristic puts the individual in an uncomfortable position, as being accepted by peers is important to almost everyone. If the individual is to thrive with respect to peer relationships, one of a limited number of options must come into play. The gifted individual can choose peer acceptance over achievement, as we have already discussed in the section on gifted underachievers. The gifted individual can "go it alone," focusing almost entirely on achievement and rejecting the peer group of the neighborhood. A third choice is to find a new peer group, one that is based more on intellectual ability or talent than on proximity and is supportive of the gifted one's efforts. A gifted tightrope walker might be able to maintain original peer group acceptance and combine it with a support group of gifted peers at school or in an after-school setting. However, no one can make this decision except the individual.

Classroom Teachers

After parents, the next most important adult figures in the lives of gifted individuals are usually the children's teachers. These may include the regular classroom teacher, special teachers in the arts or other fields, and those who become mentors (and sometimes "discoverers").

If we were to depict ideal teachers of the gifted, what characteristics or traits should those individuals have? It is *not* essential that the teachers have an IQ as high or higher than the gifted students. It *is* imperative, however, that they be experienced teachers; intelligent, enthusiastic, and knowledgeable about both the needs of their students and a variety of content fields; flexible, achievement oriented, willing to work hard, well organized, curious, able to guide rather than direct their students' activities, secure or self-confident, and willing to learn (Cropley & McLeod, 1986; Seeley, 1989a). A study comparing rural principals and teachers of the gifted in rural settings revealed a fairly similar list of competencies, adding, however, "ability to develop creative problem solving skills" and "knowledge of advanced technology" (e.g., computers), among others (K. C. Nelson & Prindle, 1992).

Some of these characteristics should be present in the individual before any special professional training, such as intellectual curiosity and emotional security, whereas other traits can be learned. The need for self-confidence or emotional security is apparent when you consider that often the student knows more than the teacher in some content area(s); the teacher has to be able to acknowledge this without feeling inadequate. The difficulty here for the gifted student can be illustrated by an editorial footnote to a letter in *Science News*:

"Your letter brings to mind a recent comment from a student subscriber. 'I value your magazine and read each issue avidly,' he wrote, but he added: 'Many of my teachers find it frustrating when I correct them in class based on information from your articles'" (Editors, 1990). Of course, it may be that the student correspondent needed to learn how to offer such corrections tactfully rather than gleefully, as some might do.

More formal qualifications may emanate from standards developed by the National Board for Professional Teaching Standards, which was established after the Carnegie report, *A Nation Prepared*, appeared in 1987 (Lathlaen, 1990). Voluntary board certification includes several competencies that are perceived as necessary for teachers of the gifted and talented, although not generally considered important for regular classroom teachers. These competencies include knowledge of special populations, including gifted students, and the broad background needed to differentiate curriculum for gifted and nongifted students. It is also possible that the board will issue specialist certification for teachers of the gifted requiring that beyond the board qualifications for regular teachers, the specialists know, for example, "how a pullout program differs from a mentor program, how to guide an independent study, or how to apply the various principles of differentiation" (Lathlaen, 1990, p. 63).

It is not enough just to know these academic procedures, however, as teacher *attitudes* can affect the ways in which such information is used. For example, in a study of teacher attitudes toward the academically gifted, Cramond and Martin (1987) found that both pre-service and in-service teachers ranked the nonstudious athletic adolescent students highest and the "brilliant-studious-nonathletic character, often the stereotype of the gifted student, . . . lowest" (p. 17). One might reasonably expect that teachers favor the former group because they feel somewhat threatened by the latter group.

There are relatively few states with teaching certificates or endorsements specifically for teachers of the gifted and talented, and only one, Louisiana, that reports having separate certificates for teachers of the talented in the fine and performing arts and for teachers of the intellectually gifted (Karnes & Whorton, 1991). However, *all* regular classroom teachers should have information on the gifted and talented as well as on other exceptional students incorporated in their undergraduate preparation. In some colleges and universities, there may be additional courses available that are focused on the gifted. More often, preparation to teach the gifted and talented is found in graduate programs, which should be competency based and include emphasis on "counseling, leadership training, cultural differences, current research, underachievers, parent/community relations, and educational technological developments" (Seeley, 1989a, p. 286).

The National Association for Gifted Children (NAGC) has developed guidelines for master's degree programs that require colleges of education and state departments of education to coordinate their efforts. The guidelines recommend that practicum experiences with gifted students should be a part of any graduate degree or certification program in this field (Feldhusen & Huffman, 1988).

There is also a variety of additional opportunities for teachers to learn the characteristics of gifted children and ways of working with these students. Outstanding among these are Confratute (CONFerence + instiTUTE), an intensive 2-week summer program organized by Joseph Renzulli at the University of Connecticut; the Creative Problem-Solving Institute sponsored by SUNY-Buffalo; and the National/State Leadership Training Institute on the Gifted and Talented (N/S LTI).

In-service courses can and should be offered by school districts in conjunction with colleges of education or educational service units with personnel that have special training in the education of the gifted and talented, such as the Intermediate Units in Pennsylvania. In addition, the NAGC and its state affiliates have annual conferences at which workshops are offered to enhance teachers' skills in this and other areas.

In what ways can teachers foster giftedness among their students? To begin, they can be alert to the individual behaviors described earlier as characteristic of gifted students. They can, for all of their students, teach those skills that enhance learning and achievement, such as focusing attention and finding problems and solving them using a variety of thinking processes, and also provide reassurance that it is human to err. For the gifted and nongifted students alike, the teacher can move away from rigidity and strict adherence to workbook assignments. As Whitmore (1988) and others have repeatedly cautioned, "If classroom conditions discourage or punish a child for expressions of giftedness (e.g., creative responses, extensive verbalization, pursuit of advanced interests), the child is even more at risk for learning problems and under-achievement in school, with behavior disorders often developing" (p. 13).

Teachers can point the way to resources and how to use them, support and encourage the student's efforts in nontraditional realms, suggest careers to be investigated, suggest goals toward which the student might work, and guide the student toward a variety of opportunities that will enhance existing abilities and offer new opportunities. Sometimes, the teacher can simply help the gifted student by being there as listener and counselor. An appropriate description of the teacher's role with respect to the gifted might be the one offered by a leader at a Creative Problem-Solving Institute several years ago: "Be a guide by the side, not a sage on stage."

There are, of course, specific assignments that will help gifted —and other—youngsters to learn to use their imaginations (e.g., Demetrulias, 1992), to transfer their skills to real-life problems (e.g., Cramond, Martin, & Shaw, 1990), and to explore new fields. Van Tassel-Baska (1991) suggests the combination of bibliotherapy, biography, journal writing, and small group work as means the teacher can use to aid gifted children in their psychosocial development as well as their cognitive development. Working with colleagues, teachers can also offer interdisciplinary courses that both challenge and appeal more to gifted—as well as some other—students because of the interweaving, for example, of history, arts, and literature (e.g., Bathgate & Connelly, 1991). From an administrative perspective, the suggestions made by these educators have an added attraction: They do not cost anything in dollars, only in effort.

Teachers can, in addition, direct students in the use of biographies, interviewing skills, and surveying techniques as means of exploring careers. This is a way in which teachers, particularly those experienced in working with gifted students, can supplement the efforts of school counselors who are confronted with too many students and not enough time to counsel them.

School Counselors

School counselors, like classroom teachers, must be sensitive to the special needs of gifted and talented students. They are the people who can facilitate implementation of IEPs, who can organize resource files from which gifted and talented students can gain helpful information, who can coordinate groups of gifted students to enhance their school experience beyond the academic, and who can mediate between these students and their parents and the school administration (Seeley, 1989a). They can also be alert to those characteristics of gifted students, especially adolescents, that may impel these youngsters to attempt suicide (Delisle, 1990; Hayes & Sloat, 1990).

In the best of possible counseling situations, counselors will have time to work with gifted (and other) students on both enhancement and prevention tasks as just suggested. In that optimal setting, and possibly even when the counseling situation is less ideal, the counselor should use available instruments to determine the approach most likely to benefit the gifted student (Griggs, 1991). This may be difficult when there are too many students assigned to each counselor.

Working with parents as well as the students is particularly critical. Some Asian and Hawaiian parents, for example, tend to be perfectionists and to exert great pressure on their children to achieve and not shame the family. The counselor's role here "is to show that biculturalism is both possible and desirable. Counselors can work with these students to support their efforts to develop traits that will help further their education and achievement, yet not alienate them from their family environments" (R. Woliver & G. M. Woliver, 1991, p. 254). At the same time, the counselor can make the parents aware of opportunities for their children that will not make them strangers in their own culture. The same task of reassuring parents that helping their gifted children to achieve will not destroy the family or the heritage is faced by counselors working with Hispanic students.

A traditional area of effort for secondary school counselors, in particular, is career guidance. With gifted youngsters, this task may arise somewhat earlier, yet be more difficult because of the paucity of "tools" on which to base advice and the relative inexperience of elementary school counselors in advising on future careers. Some gifted and talented children are clearly focused and locked into a specific field because of their unique skills, whereas others have more diffuse interests. It has been suggested that systematic examination of leisure activities, using an instrument such as the Tel-Aviv Activities Inventory, can aid the counselor (Hong, Whiston, & R. M. Milgram, 1993). Further, "Information about out-of-school activities can help teachers in their efforts to differentiate curriculum and individualize instruction in order both to interest and stimulate gifted learners . . . [and] in guiding the gifted as they choose courses, school activities, and enrichment and acceleration programs offered by many schools and communities" (Hong et al., 1993, p. 67).

One of the difficulties confronting school counselors today is that there are too many tasks to do (if one is going to do the job right) for too many students and too few counselors to do them. As economic pressures force school districts to eliminate programs and services, elementary school counselors may be among the first to go, though they are often of key importance in the young gifted student's adaptation to school. Even secondary school counselors may be reduced in force, giving those who remain heavier caseloads that will impede their efforts to work effectively with the students who need extra or nonstandard services.

Community Attitude

Parents, children, teachers, and counselors constitute only part of the community in which they function, sometimes in overlapping roles. Yet ultimately it is the community that decides what shall be taught and how much will be spent on what kinds of education, and through these decisions, the community demonstrates what it values. At times, the community is the nation as a whole, spoken for by its elected representatives in Congress. More often, however, we think of our community as the town or neighborhood in which we live or work, with its own elected officials who carry out what are the presumed popular mandates.

One problem is that there are usually conflicting mandates, as for example, between the expenditure of tax dollars locally or nationally on the needs of the aged and the needs of children. Do we care for those who have already served or for those who will serve in the future? Or attempt to do both?

The nature of education is another area of debate. Do we educate all children equally or give all children equal educational opportunity? There *is* a difference! "Educational theory and research, money and expertise will not improve our schools until citizens decide to take seriously what is happening to the children in their community, and take action" (Csikszentmihalyi, 1993, p. 51). It is up to the community, whether we are looking at the neighborhood that manages the local school or the larger society that establishes the climate from which smaller communities take their cues to decide how to answer these questions.

> While public and private rhetoric is full of pieties about the importance of children, statistics about their actual conditions tell quite a different story. . . . On several counts the condition of our children seems to be getting worse from year to year, decade after decade. . . . Those who survive learn less in school than do their peers in most comparable countries, and are, therefore, less well prepared for a productive adulthood. (Csikszentmihalyi, 1993, pp. 31-32)

The community is represented in educational matters by its elected school board members, although members of the community frequently attend board meetings to press their concerns and argue their perspectives. Community voices are also raised in the press, and what is printed in the popular as well as professional media affects community attitudes—virtually a circular effect. Within a 6-week period (October 15 to November 28, 1992), five articles in just two newspapers (the *New York Times* and the *Philadelphia Inquirer*) argued the issue of special education for the gifted (see Figure 5.1). About 5 months later, another story played the familiar theme of

Education for the Gifted, Seen as a Luxury, Faces Cutbacks
- *The New York Times*, Nov. 28, 1992

CHALLENGE TO PROGRAMS FOR THE GIFTED
- *The Philadelphia Inquirer*, October 15, 1992

Should Tracking Be Derailed?
- *The New York Times (Education Life)*, Nov. 1, 1992

Mix, Don't Match
- *The New York Times (Education Life)*, Nov. 1, 1992

Selecting The Smart Set
- *The New York Times (Education Life)*, Nov. 1, 1992

Figure 5.1. Headlines and the Gifted

elitism. The headline read: "Schools' tracks and democracy—Sorting students by performance: Efficiency or elitism?" (Strum, 1993).

What is not discussed in these stories, and certainly is not apparent in the headlines, is the fact that it is not tracking per se that is bad, undemocratic, elitist, or even beneficial; it is the way in which tracking is handled and perceived. Rigid, across-the-board tracking rarely benefits even the gifted students, as their patterns of strengths and weaknesses are as unique as their physical development. Flexibility in placement, however, where students most able in English composition are together, but may be redistributed in math or science or social studies classes, is far more appropriate in providing educational opportunities even though it demands greater administrative attention to scheduling.

Popular views of the gifted, modified from time to time, include links to emotional instability (if not mental illness) and jealousy that sometimes escalates to resentment and hostility. They are seen as having more than their share of ability, so why should they be given special attention in the schools? As Gallagher put it, these views "fit into a primitive concept of *equity*. That is, if a person has a great many talents and gifts in one area, it is only 'fair' that they should have some disability, as well, to balance it off" (1990, p. 202). This is equivalent to saying that a Miss America should have a chronic illness or be grossly inept in some other area to offset her physical beauty or that an Olympic medal winner should be given a handicap in future competitions. Vonnegut depicted such a situation in the United States late in the 21st century, attributing its success to the "unceasing vigilance of agents of the U.S. Handicapper General" (1991, p. 683). (Note that schoolchildren may participate in an exercise of this kind, designed to acquaint them with and make them sensitive to the handicaps of old age—petroleum jelly on eyeglasses, for instance, or a weight placed on one leg. This is entirely different from the weighted handicap bags, ear buzzers, and ugly face masks worn by the gifted and talented in Vonnegut's "Harrison Bergeron.")

The inanity of this idea of equity should be immediately apparent to most people. Similarly, then, the handicapping of gifted youth in their education in the name of equity should be quickly dismissed, partly because of the weak reasoning behind the attitude and partly, as stated earlier, because these youths are a major community and national resource. As Barber (1992) wrote, "Education need not begin with equally adept students, because education is itself the equalizer. Equality is achieved not by handicapping the swiftest, but by assuring the less advantaged a comparable opportunity. 'Comparable' ... does not mean identical" (p. 13).

6 The Special Case of Gifted Females

Perhaps the problems confronted by gifted females can best be illustrated by Lembke's (1992) anecdotal description of Sally. Sally, a sixth grader who always did all her work perfectly, had no playmates at recess and appeared to be resented by her classmates. During the school year, Lembke gave one test on which no one, not even Sally, received a perfect score.

> As I returned the papers, I commented on each child's error. When I called Sally's name every head in the class popped up; all eyes and ears focused on Sally and me as we discussed the error.
> Sally looked at me and burst into a beautiful smile as she clutched the paper and walked back to her seat. All eyes followed her. To this day I am not sure whether that was a real error or whether Sally made it on purpose. At recess the other girls invited Sally to play ball. (p. 2)

This is but one example of what Horner (1970) described as fear of success, which tens of thousands of gifted girls have experienced over many decades.

"Are You a Girl or a Grind?"

According to Schwartz (1991), there are several indications of the need to study gifted girls as a separate subgroup of the gifted population. One needs to look, for example, at the barriers confronting gifted girls that affect realization of their potential. Some of these barriers are shared equally with gifted boys; these include personal problems of self-motivation, the ambivalence of society with respect to gifted students, and the lack of opportunity or encouragement. Others, such as parental expectations, sex role conflicts, fear of failure, fear of success, and attribution, more often have impact primarily on girls.

This situation is not limited to the United States. Ayles (1992) reported at an international conference that

> this pattern of unjustifiably low expectations, lack of confidence, social pressure to underachieve and a bias away from science and technology, *established during the first years of education in school* [italics added], is reflected in the higher stages of education. Women students in the UK are still underrepresented in universities and polytechnics, although they are well represented in lower level courses of further education. (p. 158)

Similarly, Kwan (1993) reports on Chinese gifted adolescent females in Singapore who were more depressed about boy-girl relationships than their male gifted peers and who had less parental support than their brothers or male peers. The exception to the latter situation occurred when the mothers of gifted girls had themselves had university education. As Kwan hypothesized, these mothers

> can conceivably act as role models who, in the eyes of their gifted daughters, have been able to reconcile academic achievement with femininity. This necessarily implies that exposure to and actual interaction with live role models may help gifted girls to resolve their own sex-role conflicts, thus leading to an enhanced adjustment. (p. 173)

Although Kwan disagrees with the need to teach gifted girls ways in which to deal with multiple concurrent roles (pp. 175-176), this comment on mothers as role models seems to belie such a negative view.

"Are you a girl or a grind?" is a question that still confronts gifted girls, especially in regular classrooms. Although there is somewhat more respect accorded gifted girls today, the conflict between social peer pressure and academic talent persists from preadolescence through early adulthood. These girls, like their gifted male counterparts, are faced with academic stagnation in regular classes but social ostracism if they do too well as students.

More than 50 years ago, Margaret Mead (1935) asserted that "the boy is taught to achieve, the girl to prove that she doesn't achieve, will never achieve. The same threat hangs over the nonachieving boy and the achieving girl, the threat that he or she will never be chosen by a member of the opposite sex" (p. 302). Or, as Callahan (1980) put it, "It appears that many young girls and women have been enculturated to the extent that they fear that they will be rejected socially or be considered unfeminine if they appear to be too bright or too competent" (p. 17). Fortunately, some of this fear is being reduced, if slowly, as legal prohibitions against discrimination in hiring are enforced, although "glass ceilings" are still prevalent in many occupations and companies. "Precisely because the gifted girl may perceive incoming 'messages' as conflicting, it is necessary to provide guidance and counseling to her that may differ from that recommended for gifted learners, in general" (Schwartz, 1991, pp. 143-144).

Parents and Gifted Daughters

In an informal survey of 10 parents who had at least one gifted daughter, it was interesting to note that 4 of them found the daughter exciting or interesting to be around, only 1 said that the daughter "scares me with her ability," and 7 felt that the child could achieve more. These parents had a total of 19 children, of whom 13 were girls (with 10 girls identified as gifted, 2 possibly gifted; 2 sons identified as gifted; and the remaining children too young to be identified). Queried about hopes for their gifted daughters, seven of the parents responded with some version of the wish that the daughter would "make the choices best for her"; two hoped she would marry and have children *and* have a career; and an additional three expressed the hope that she would "go for broke" in the career field of her choice. Perhaps the fact that these parents were attending a conference session on gifted daughters made them a somewhat more biased subject group than might be found in the larger community, but the fact is that they were positively oriented toward an all-around adult life for their very able daughters (Schwartz, 1987).

Are these parents unusual? They appear to regard having a gifted daughter more as a pleasure than a plague, but this attitude may change with the daughter's age. For many parents, their attitude toward a gifted daughter may depend upon whether they would have preferred having a son or whether this daughter is more talented than the son they do have. Parental behavior can reinforce sex role stereotypes, and their priorities will certainly be communicated to their daughters. What do they hold as primarily important—academic standing? Social acceptance? Well-roundedness?

As one example, leaders in the women's movement in the 1960s through the 1980s ($N = 7$) placed considerable importance on the contributions of *their* parents to their adult lives. These were women who would be regarded as gifted in social intelligence and leadership qualities as well as academically (each had earned at least a master's degree). The parents served as role models, strongly supported their daughters' strengths and abilities, and held high expectations for their daughters' ultimate achievements in life (Astin & Leland, 1991). Grandparents were also critical figures, with grandmothers often serving as models of strength and as sources of wisdom. Of course, some of the parents combined their support messages with messages about marriage, but Astin and Leland's subjects reported that these mixed messages "had the effect of making daughters more self-determined and more autonomous" (1991, p. 46).

If parents truly want to help their gifted daughters to be self-actualizing as they mature, then they must allow the girls to express and to follow their own preferences (within the limits of safety). They need to allow the girl time alone when she can dream, explore and develop new interests, set personal goals, and evaluate her own performance. They can help to expose her to the world of work (as in the Ms. Foundation-sponsored "Take your daughter to work" day) and to the possibility of successfully coordinating family life and achievement outside the family or choosing one option over another. Parents can also help their gifted daughters to have a balanced perspective regarding their self-image, their peer relationships, and their talents.

Gender-Specific Barriers

The typical girl pupil, whether she is gifted or not, is usually expected to behave in certain ways. The pattern to which she is expected to conform includes being relatively quiet rather than outspoken, being neat, being on time, and being unquestioningly obedient. The girl who is assertive, who seeks challenges, and who is high aspiring and high achieving is perceived as atypical (i.e., "masculine") by her teachers and possibly as less socially desirable by them (Handel, 1982). This can affect the teacher's behavior, often in a negative direction, toward the nonconformist girl.

It is important to recognize that one's philosophical stance affects interaction with and decisions made with respect to the education of gifted girls (Higham & Navarre, 1984). We are guided by the positions we hold, such as belief in the innate inferiority of women, equality of males and females, superiority of women, or differential egalitarianism. As educators, we cannot directly affect the genetic endowment that gifted girls have, but we can and do affect the experiences and opportunities they have. We must, therefore, examine our own biases and those of the people with whom we and gifted girls interact if we are to respond appropriately to the girls' needs. (These pages are being written early in the Clinton administration. Some people respect and admire the competence of the president's wife, Hillary Rodham Clinton, and applaud his assignment of her to executive chores as well as traditional First Lady duties. Other people clearly resent her accomplishments, her abilities, and her nontraditional status. Clinton's first nominee for the post of Attorney General, Zoe Baird, attracted similar ambivalence when it was noted that her salary with an insurance company was $500,000 a year. The cultural stereotypes for females die hard.)

See the Gifted Girls in School

Once outside the family, perhaps in day care or nursery school, the precocious little girl may face her first challenges. Not fitting the stereotype of playing in the cooking corner, speaking quietly, and staying clean may generate teacher/caretaker criticisms that turn off her curiosity, creativity, and nonconformity. Teacher acceptance continues to be important through kindergarten and the primary grades, so that the flowering of these traits will again depend upon the personal prejudices and flexibility of the teachers.

One study directed questions to a group of multiethnic girls in Grades 3-6 who had been identified as having "high potential" and asked them to identify the problems with which they were confronted. They identified six areas:

1. Achievement versus affiliation
2. Silence versus bragging
3. Failure versus perfection
4. Media beauty versus marginality
5. Passive versus aggressive
6. Conforming versus being punished (Bell, 1989)

Bell concluded that "Girls often perceive dilemmas as either/or situations in which their options are limited and their values ignored.

This double bind leads many highly capable girls to lose self-confidence, minimize their abilities, downplay their achievements, and jeopardize their future options" (p. 127). As part of Bell's project, the girls collectively wrestled with these situations and worked out ways in which they could reduce the problems comfortably. The support group format apparently reduced their feelings of having unique problems that rendered them helpless and lead to underachievement and negative self-concepts.

Given long-enduring gender stereotypes, is there a need to pay special attention to gifted girls as separate from gifted students in general? Navarre (1980) postulated that we should do so, offering a number of suggestions that included support groups of and for gifted girls (as in Bell's project), same-sex models (especially in nontraditional occupations), and compensatory instruction in math and the sciences (where girls tend to score lower in performance). She later expanded upon these ideas, notably adding that girls may need some sex-segregated classes where they can "shine" with less anxiety, and more informed career counseling (Higham & Navarre, 1984).

Several of these needs, as well as better counseling for girls, become apparent in Halpern's (1992) study of gender differences in abilities. Some of her studies suggest unusual pairings of factors, such as

> the finding that scores on tests of spatial abilities and verbal abilities depend on sex *and* whether an individual is right- or left-handed.... At least among subjects with high reasoning ability, left-handed males performed poorer on spatial abilities tests than right-handed males, but left-handed males had the advantage over right-handed males on tests of verbal abilities. (p. 239)

Other studies she reports suggest that what may have been thought to be a biological gender-related difference a generation ago (e.g., spatial ability) is clearly not, as women in recent years have entered the workforce in architecture, engineering, and other scientific fields with considerable success (p. 242). As Halpern is careful to point out, biological makeup and psychosocial environment are so intertwined in any given individual that it is impossible to determine which is the more important factor in individual differences. This leads her to conclude that

> it is clear from the current research that biology is not destiny. Even if biological differences underlie some portion of

the cognitive differences, there is ample evidence to conclude that under environmental conditions that encourage the total intellectual development of males and females, the size of the sex differential in cognitive abilities can be reduced, and possibly even eliminated. (p. 249)

Motivation and the Gifted Girl

Using a multidimensional model that included personal, environmental, and background factors, Farmer (1987) reviewed several studies to explore the reasons for gender differences in motivation. She subdivided motivation into aspiration, mastery, and career commitment and tested her model on more than 1,800 adolescents representative of the black, Hispanic, and white populations. A colleague used an adapted model to replicate her test with 212 young adults. In the area of aspiration, Farmer found that background factors had an indirect effect on gender differences:

> These young women's high Aspiration was enhanced by perceived Support for Women Working and by Teacher Support. For young men, a Competitive self-concept, Ability Attributions, and Parent Support enhanced Aspiration. These gender differences point to the important role of school and other environment influences on gender differences in Aspiration motivation. (p. 7)

Interestingly, she also found that

> high school Aspiration motivation is not a good predictor of adult achievement.... What it tells us is that not all highly motivated students achieve equally as adults, and that this is significantly more true for females and minorities. Something happens between high school and adult employment to reduce the status attainment of these groups. (p. 7)

The area of Mastery motivation appeared to be most strongly influenced by personal variables, but the effect of environmental factors was again stronger for young females than young males. To Farmer, this "finding suggests that if Mastery motivation is to be enhanced for young women, supportive programs in the school and the home, as well as within the society at large, could make a difference" (p. 7).

Career commitment was also more influenced by personal factors than by environment and background factors.

> This was the only motivation dimension for which female students had significantly higher scores compared to males. Career motivation was influenced for females by Math Ability and several personal variables (i.e., Expressive, Independent, Cooperative, Competitive, Effort Attributions, Intrinsic Values, and Homemaking). The personal influences were all in the positive direction, with the exception of Homemaking, which had a negative influence on Career motivation for these young women. (p. 7)

Certainly these personal factors are affected by both parents and teachers, as well as by others significant in an individual's preadolescent life. The adults provide the models, the examples for social learning, the positive reinforcement of some behaviors and not others. One specific illustration is in the area of science achievement, where males tend to gain an advantage over females in the 2-year period from seventh to ninth grade. The interest in science among early adolescent girls is thought to diminish for a variety of reasons; it was found to occur even earlier among daughters of separated parents, presumably because the separated mothers were showing a model more typical of the female stereotype than mothers from intact marriages (T. E. Smith, 1992). Lewis (1985) commented that

> the way in which schools are organized and society's perception that math and science rest in the male domain have a decided impact on the self-perception of females. Subliminal messages transmitted by the media and the school reinforce the *appropriateness* of computer technology for specific individuals. For example, photographs and promotional materials of computer software and hardware depict more males as teachers, consumers, and students. (pp. 129-130)

Further, she wrote, parents were apparently more willing to invest larger sums in computer camps or schools for their sons than their daughters, again perpetuating a sexual stereotype.

Attribution, Anxiety, and Achievement

Dealing with attributions for success and failure calls for helping the gifted girl (or any child) to develop an internal locus of control. That simply means that she is aware that her successes are due to her ability or effort and that her failures, although possibly due to factors beyond her control, may also be due to her own *lack* of effort

(Schwartz, 1987). In helping to develop this internal locus, especially with gifted children, it is important to make them aware at the same time that to err is human and being gifted does not mean having to be perfect in every task or at all times (Schwartz, 1991).

The fear of failure that accompanies expectations of perfect performance, internally or externally based, is as harmful to the gifted girl's accomplishments in the classroom as is the fear of success model put forward by Horner (1970). In the former case, the girl becomes afraid to risk revealing lack of knowledge or skill, so she refuses to venture into new areas or to try new activities. If she doesn't try, obviously she can't fail (i.e., be seen as less than perfect). If she doesn't try, however, she may also miss opportunities for learning, for achievement, for awards, for self-actualization. Accordingly, teachers as well as parents must be conscious of the messages they convey, such as "to take risks is unwise," or "girls do not have what it takes to work in a specific field." The field usually meant in this message is mathematics related. Girls have been given this message so often and with such conviction that they tend to believe it. They develop math anxiety even when they are perfectly capable of succeeding with the most challenging math courses and choose not to take them. If they practice such avoidance in high school, they will not be prepared to take courses in college that will prepare them for employment in technical fields—thus fulfilling the prediction once again.

Fear of success, on the other hand, is tied more to nonacademic factors than is fear of failure. Here, gifted girls *know* that they can achieve at a high level, but are afraid that this will make them unpopular with their peers—as happened with Sally earlier in this chapter. Lack of popularity with boys is even more threatening, so the gifted girl in the primary classroom learns to mute her voice and her ability as she moves higher in the grades and approaches adolescence.

For the gifted girl's parents, the conflict may begin during their daughter's early adolescent years, when they "want her to be happy, and to spare her the pain of being socially different. They begin to praise her more for appearance than before, while showing greater interest in her social life—perhaps trivializing her intellectual achievement" (B. A. Kerr, 1985, p. 105). The task of reconciling academic abilities and interests with the areas of excellence traditionally perceived as appropriate for women poses yet another problem for gifted girls. "After all, some may ask, how much history or economics or physics can the gifted woman use in her role as wife and mother?" (Schwartz, 1980, p. 113).

Even as the gifted girl is encouraged to pursue her interests while in school, it seems unrealistic, inefficient, and grossly unfair to erect barriers that inhibit her using her knowledge in the marketplace after graduation. That potential source of intellectual or artistic frustration is almost certain to inhibit the classroom performance of a gifted girl. It also plays into the hands of those, usually males, who even today assert that a college education is wasted on girls.

Effects of Giftedness on Nonacademic Life Areas

Concerns about the negative effects of acceleration on the social interaction of gifted females, a common anxiety among parents, appear to be unwarranted. According to Richardson and Benbow (1990), for those female students who had engaged in grade acceleration "no differential effects of acceleration (grade or subject matter) on social-emotional adjustment were found" (p. 468).

Looking at gifted adolescent girls, it is apparent that parent-child communication plays an important role in the girls' self-concept as competent or not. "Daughters who enjoy more positive and open communication with their parents have higher perceptions of their competence in a wide range of areas" (Callahan, Cornell, & Loyd, 1990, p. 265). This was true for both parents, although "better communication with mothers was associated with more favorable self-perceptions of job competence and romantic appeal" whereas closer relationships with fathers was negatively correlated with self-views of athletic competence (Callahan et al., 1990, p. 265). The importance of good parent-child communication is, of course, not limited to gifted adolescent females.

Despite the admission of females to previously all-male colleges, and vice versa, there are still arguments for sex-segregated schools and colleges as having special benefits for girls. Indeed, just prior to becoming a coeducational school in the mid-1970s, Hunter College High School's "single-sex" advocates,

> enlightened by feminism, . . . had come to see what Hunter girls had always known: that single-sex education had tremendous advantages for women. . . . At a single-sex school, the girls did not feel like second-class citizens, or fall silent in classroom discussion, or develop much anxiety, or settle for running for student government secretary. (Stone, 1992, p. 72)

There are also usually more models available at single-sex schools for less traditional career paths. At the college level, for example, a high degree of interest in chemistry at Mount Holyoke over many years has created "a climate in which chemistry was a typical, rather than a nontraditional, career path" (Shmurak & Handler, 1992, p. 342). Half of the subjects called "Instigators" by Astin and Leland (1991) had graduated from women's colleges, places where they gained a sense of women's roles in major social movements as well as the opportunity to be leaders themselves (pp. 55-56).

The importance of locating suitable mentors for gifted girls cannot be overstated. They may be accustomed to seeing female teachers, but female engineers? Female accountants? Female business executives? Female clergy? Female judges? Gifted girls need to see that females can do almost anything.

Girls and Creative Ability

As we earlier considered creativity, or creative potential, as one facet of giftedness, it seems appropriate to ask whether males and females differ in creative ability, and if so, why. Although there may be some biological differences that affect creative potential, Abra and Valentine-French (1991) note that "women have often excelled in fields for which formal preparation has been widely accessible (literary arts require only literacy), or unnecessary (dance grows from a basic ability, movement), but rarely in science, mathematics, or music, which all demand extensive, hitherto highly restricted formal training" (p. 246). Further, historical evidence suggests that on the one hand, women have not had access to those fields that were supported by religious patronage, such as architecture or composition for the organ or choir, whereas on the other hand, they were as subject to attacks on their character as their brother artists. However, they were less eligible for the marriage market as a result of such slanderous attacks than were the males.

Girls have certainly had fewer models for creative or academic achievement than boys, with the rare exceptions that today they can look back and up to Marie Curie or Maria Mitchell in the sciences, Margaret Mead and Ruth Benedict in anthropology, or Berthe Morisot or Mary Cassatt in fine art. The lack of a model for social learning or of reinforcement for creative activity (in the Skinnerian format) have long worked against whatever gifts and personal characteristics (e.g., intrinsic motivation, self-confidence) girls have had. Their persistence in pursuing self-imposed tasks rather than parent-preferred premarital behaviors is perceived as stubbornness, the negative face of persistence. Criticized as nonconformist and too independent, the female who hears her own drummer, even today, is also berated as being selfish, possibly guilty of penis envy, uncaring about others' (notably parents') approval, and so on (Abra & Valentine-French, 1991).

To what extent the feminist movement in the last quarter of the 20th century will reduce the conflict and increase female creativity cannot yet be determined. There has been, however, some movement at least since the early 1980s toward recognizing women artists in books of art history together with the founding of a national museum devoted to women in the arts in Washington, D.C., and more exhibits and concerts devoted to women's creative productions as distinct from men's.

B. A. Kerr (1985), in examining the lives of seven eminent women, acknowledged several key principles in guiding gifted girls, including childhood mentoring, individualized instruction, and encouragement. However, she concluded that the traits and behaviors that essentially characterized these women (Marie Curie, Eleanor Roosevelt, Georgia O'Keeffe, Margaret Mead, Gertrude Stein, Maya Angelou, and Beverly Sills) as eminent in adulthood were "the determined refusal to acknowledge limitations of gender, an ability to combine roles, a strong sense of one's personal identity, taking responsibility for oneself, and a mission in life" (p. v). Some of these characteristics we hope all youths will gain as they develop into adults; others may be more easily associated with the gifted and talented or the more willful and energetic. Refusing to "acknowledge limitations of gender," however, should be an appropriate goal for all educators.

Counseling Gifted Girls

Years ago, vocational interest tests such as the Strong-Campbell Vocational Interest Inventory and others had no provision for scoring girls' responses for medicine, law, engineering, accounting, or college teaching. (Of course, boys could not be scored for some occupations either, such as nursing, bookkeeping, elementary school teaching, etc.) Although antidiscrimination laws have reduced flagrant abuses of career guidance for girls and have stimulated the updating and restandardization of vocational interest tests to be more in tune with today's world, guidance counselors themselves must be similarly in tune with the fact that girls can enter any field if they have the proper preparation and credentials.

Of particular concern here is the need to encourage gifted girls to take advanced science and mathematics courses in high school to enable them to move toward any major in college or any career, as well as to become sufficiently computer literate to be able to use this valuable tool. To reach this goal, girls need to acquire a more positive attitude toward mathematics and the sciences. Although this is a problem generally for gifted girls, Lamb and Daniels (1993) proposed that it may be especially so for gifted girls in rural settings, where there are more intense pressures for social conformity. Accordingly, they introduced an intervention program for gifted girls in Grades 4-7 designed to change their attitudes toward math, expand their awareness of career options in the field, and teach problem-solving strategies. Differences between the experimental and control groups at pretesting on the Mathematics Attitude Inventory were not significant, but were highly significant on five out of six subtest scores, as well as total scores, at the posttesting 18 weeks later. As these researchers concluded, "If young gifted girls are to reach their potential mathematically, they must possess positive attitudes. The evidence from this study indicates that math attitudes of gifted females can be influenced. Thus, gifted females . . . can develop potential that will broaden career choices" (p. 517).

In addition, all-day workshops such as the Math Options project at Penn State's Ogontz and Delaware campuses (sponsored by Bell of Pennsylvania) seek to interest girls in careers involved with or dependent upon mathematics. Although not limited to the mathematically gifted, it is reasonably assumed that most of the seventh-grade participants are good math students who need encouragement and models in this area. The girls spend a day on campus meeting professional women from mathematics, science, engineering, technology, and related fields and interacting with them in a variety of workshops. Concurrent sessions are also held for their teachers, to increase their awareness of the importance of mathematics for girls.

There is also a need for counselors to assist their students of both sexes to become aware that planning is necessary for combining work, family, and community involvement (Perrone, 1986). Too often, it has been noted, only female students have had this issue raised, and more often in a negative way than as a constructive effort. Although not every girl, not even every gifted girl, has to build a career, "in this day of high divorce rates, increasing options to choose the unmarried and/or childless life, and challenging opportunities in a wide array of fields, the gifted girl needs also to be prepared for economic independence as an adult" (Schwartz, 1991, p. 157).

However well academically prepared, she also needs the self-confidence to move toward her chosen field. Her teachers and counselors, as well as her parents, should help her to overcome the negative effects of gender stereotypes, find ways around gender-based barriers, and activate her potential abilities and her interests in as favorable a setting as possible. If, even in the age of increased feminism, the gifted girl has learned to be reticent to ward off negative comments, it may be that she will need assertiveness training in order to be identified at the high school, college, or career level.

Conclusion

Looking at the gifted girl from the perspective of what is best for her as an individual, it should be self-evident that parents, teachers, and counselors need to nurture her self-confidence, her motivation, her interests, and her abilities if she is to be adequately prepared to make choices and decisions for her life—if she is, in other words, to be able to function as a mature and independent adult. Looking at the gifted girl from the perspective of national needs, how dare anyone say or imply that her talents should not be fostered and her gifts should not be used in socially constructive ways simply because she is a female?

7 Educational Options

As we have seen, though they tend to share certain personality characteristics, gifted and talented students vary in personal background, environmental influences, areas of giftedness, and opportunities. The question becomes one of meeting their distinctive needs during the years they are in school. In what ways might we best do this? Answers to the question must be in the plural because of a variety of factors: resources of the school district in staff and dollars, the number of students involved in any geographic area, and community attitudes, among others. Overall, however, according to Sato (1988), "To serve the gifted/talented most effectively, curriculum must be appropriately differentiated, articulated kindergarten through grade 12, sequential in content to be assimilated and skills to be acquired, substantive in subject matter, and linked meaningfully to the regular curriculum" (p. 93).

These program characteristics are included in the Standards for Programs Involving the Gifted and Talented developed by The Association for the Gifted, a division of the Council for Exceptional Children (1989). Incorporating them into a school district's format entails long-term planning with an overarching statement of goals that is then supported by specific curriculum and annual objectives, including "skeletal unit plans" for every unit in every course. Such a detailed approach may seem overwhelming to many teachers and administrators, yet it does provide a useful framework for a district's program design and an appropriate parallel to IEPs.

Of particular concern is how to handle gifted students at the middle school level, the preteen and early adolescent years when children are becoming more conscious of peer relationships and more desirous of peer acceptance. Frequently these youngsters have much stronger academic self-concepts than social self-concepts, which suggests a need to develop proactive programs in this area (Ross & Parker, 1980). There is controversy between those who would emphasize the developmental changes through chronologically heterogeneous grouping and those who would stress the advanced cognitive/intellectual levels of gifted students through acceleration or other options (Sicola, 1990). As we have already seen, however, many gifted youngsters are also more socially and emotionally mature than their age peers and actually feel more comfortable with classmates a year or two older than themselves. This once again points to the need for individualizing programs for these students while also providing opportunities for them to interact with their age peers when it is appropriate.

One way to categorize the educational options available for gifted and talented students is to divide them into "replacement systems" and "supplementary systems" (R. M. Milgram & Goldring, 1991). "Replacement" options are those offered during the regular school day in place of regular class activities for some period of time, whereas "supplements" are offered outside of regular school hours, including on weekends and during vacations. Thus, "replacement systems" would include:

1. Enrichment or acceleration in the regular classroom
2. Part-time/pullout special classes
3. Special classes
4. Full-time special schools (selective admission based on high IQ scores and grades)
5. Full-time specialized schools (magnet schools for gifted students in specific academic disciplines)
6. Full- and part-time special schools (including residential)

The "supplementary systems," on the other hand, include:

1. Concurrent or dual university enrollment
2. Classes sponsored by universities (afternoon, weekend, summer, vacation periods)
3. Classes in public settings (afternoon, weekend, summer, vacation periods)
4. Internships and mentor programs (R. M. Milgram & Goldring, 1991, pp. 26-28)

Another way to divide the educational options is by delivery systems, which overlap some of the previous listings. In this format, the principal educational options for working with gifted students are:

1. Mainstreaming, with or without modifications within the classroom
2. Enrichment programs
3. Homogeneous classes or schools (e.g., sex segregated or IQ segregated)
4. Acceleration, gradual or radical
5. Mentoring
6. Independent study
7. Distance education
8. Summer, weekend, or other brief programs

Each of these will be discussed in the coming pages, with relevant research cited. It should be kept in mind, however, that the most appropriate programs for gifted students, both in general and specifically, may include some combination of these possibilities. K. B. Rogers and Kimpston (1992), for example, list 11 types of what they call "Accelerative Practice," some of which might more appropriately be called "alternative paths."

No matter which of these schema is used for categorizing the options, one common element is basic. Appropriate curricula for the gifted should modify one or more of the following facets of learning: the rate of learning, the level of difficulty of the content to be learned, the quantity and quality of what is to be learned, and the self-direction of the learners.

Mainstreaming

Mainstreaming refers to the "normal" classroom—without segregation by ability or gender or handicap. It may also refer to a class with a heterogeneous population. Any allowance made for individual differences depends to a great extent on the attitude as well as the skill of the classroom teacher, whether at the elementary or the secondary level. School district policy, of course, also has an effect on the ways in which the academically gifted are perceived and taught within this setting.

The academically gifted youngster who is assigned to the top reading group in a third-grade class and who has to keep to the pace of the others in that group, despite a sixth-grade reading ability, is likely to become frustrated, stymied, bored, and depending on personality variables, withdrawn, negativistic, or uninterested in further learning. It is at this point that the gifted child may become a "gifted underachiever," although there may also be others in the class who have learned to function in this way to meet their own needs. Under such circumstances, the teacher is well advised to pay attention to the factors contributing to such negative performance (Supplee, 1990).

If held to the class pace and assignments, the very able student is likely to complete the work well ahead of others and then possibly be assigned additional pages of *the same work* or be criticized for daydreaming. If assigned to help less able classmates, the gifted student can feel either useful (for a time) or exploited and may be resented by peers (as seen in the example of "Sally" in the last chapter) or become resentful. Among high-ability students, peer tutoring is seen as a fairer practice than other practices suggested to them (e.g., having fast learners wait for the slower ones who may never complete an assignment, enrichment, acceleration), especially among younger gifted children (Thorkildsen, 1993). This perception changes as the gifted students grow older, however.

Cooperative learning, in which the gifted work with less able students as a team, is often urged as an efficacious way to manage heterogeneous classes. A small sample of middle school gifted students experienced in cooperative learning, however, stated that they had difficulty understanding why others couldn't grasp material that they found simple and resented having to explain content to classmates who were not interested in it (Matthews, 1992). They did not resent working in a group, but they found it less frustrating if those with whom they were teamed had abilities on their level, although possibly with strengths in different interest or content areas. Under these circumstances, they felt that they could learn something new and maintain their positive attitudes. In some cases, four to six of these gifted students can be placed in a "cluster group" within the larger class and work together at their level on tasks designed by the teacher, who has had special training for working with gifted students (Winebrenner & Devlin, 1993).

Another common practice, especially in the elementary grades, is to have the gifted child assume some quasi-teacher responsibilities. If assigned to messenger and monitoring duties because he/she has completed work quickly, or to help with bulletin boards, the gifted youngster may again feel put upon once the novelty of these activities has expired. There is also the danger of being perceived as a teacher's pet, which adds to the psychosocial distance between the gifted student and classmates.

Individualizing instruction and assignments for the varied abilities of a heterogeneous class takes a great deal of time, effort, knowledge, and resources. (Unfortunately, not all teachers are willing to expend the first two of these and they may not have an ample supply of the latter two.) Optimally, the classroom teacher will be able to work cooperatively with a specialist teacher of the gifted, and together this team can design effective learning experiences for the gifted and talented learners. An excellent example of such cooperative effort can be found in N. C. Milgram (1989).

At the elementary level, the energetic teacher may set up reading stations, science corners, and other alternative activities for the gifted student to use when assignments are completed. The teacher may also use an outcomes-based approach to reduce the tedium of doing pages of workbook/textbook problems when the youngster is already knowledgeable in a content area. That is, in effect, the teacher says "show me" that the competence is there and then allows the student to proceed to more independent work. A number of helpful suggestions along this line are provided by Colon and Treffinger (1980).

Individualized independent learning activities are one key to encouraging the gifted to remain interested in school tasks. Mulhern (1978), for example, suggests utilizing "primary and secondary source documents as a means to obtain first hand information on current problems and topics of interest" (p. 5). In reading such documents, the student not only may gain a deeper understanding and knowledge of the roots of a current problem, but also may be able to analyze differences in the ways language is used between, for example, the 18th century and the late 20th. A student talented in art might be able to trace the development of a particular movement or emphasis in painting or sculpture through several decades or centuries. The information gained may be used as the basis for a term paper or as part of a class presentation, perhaps giving a deeper dimension to a class play.

"Curriculum compacting," one of the techniques suggested by Reis and Renzulli (1992), is described by these educators as "organized common sense." In other words, once students are identified as having mastered the class curriculum, they are given the opportunity to participate in activities that will enhance their skills in a content area by means other than review and practice.

Even these activities may be insufficient for a gifted student. One group of gifted sixth graders, for example, reported that teachers and peers in the mainstreamed class, as compared with those in a class for gifted, had unrealistic and sometimes unfair expectations of them (Clinkenbeard, 1991). They felt that the regular class setting deprived *them* of appropriate opportunities to learn. Depending upon the policies enunciated at the state level and the resources of the local district, it may be necessary, as well as appropriate, to turn to one or more of the other educational options.

Enrichment

Enrichment "refers to qualitatively different sorts of programs" offered to gifted students that expose them to more of a variety of content in greater depth (Feldhusen, 1991, p. 133). The student might begin the study of a foreign language in second grade, or learn about and write different forms of poetry in fifth grade, or read biographies of artists of a particular era either in a pullout enrichment class or as a home assignment. There is no reason why enrichment activities have to be limited to the gifted, however, as Tannenbaum (1983) pointed out and Renzulli (1984) demonstrated. Enrichment activities are attempts to meet the educational goal of individualizing instruction for *all* students, but educators must recognize that some learning experiences "can help gifted children to achieve excellence but would be excessively demanding on the nongifted" (Tannenbaum, 1983, p. 374). A few examples of enrichment programs follow.

In Renzulli's (1977) Enrichment Triad, there are three types or stages of enrichment: General Exploratory and Group Training Activities (Type I), Group Training Activities (Type II), and Investigations of Real Problems (Type III). Through the Type I activities, students are exposed to a wide variety of potential fields of study through interest centers, field trips, meetings with adult practitioners in a field, and other activities and are expected to select a field of special interest at the conclusion of their exploration. At the second stage, they are taught a variety of higher level thinking processes; and in the third stage, they have the opportunity to apply these techniques to real problems.

The Milford Futurology Program, designed for gifted ninth graders, met for one period daily for one semester. The purpose of the program was to assist these students "to develop the skills, the perspective, and the characteristics necessary to deal effectively with change" (Fletcher & Wooddell, 1980, p. 16). In fact, summative evaluations indicated that the program was successful in that the youngsters tended to become more self-actualized and inner directed.

A Program for Academic and Creative Enrichment (PACE), based on the Purdue Three-Stage Model for Gifted Education, was offered to more than 200 potentially or identified gifted students in Grades 3-6 of eight elementary schools in Lafayette, Indiana (Kolloff &

Feldhusen, 1984). Broad goals for the program "included the development of basic creative thinking and problem solving abilities; the development of higher level thinking skills, independent study, and research skills; and the development and maintenance of positive self-concepts through interaction with other gifted students" (p. 53). These goals were to be met through two 1-hour sessions per week over a 6-month period. Compared with an equal number of peers similarly identified but not in the PACE program, the goals in creative thinking were met at a significant level, but self-concepts, as measured, were not affected either positively or negatively.

Frequently the elementary level enrichment program offers opportunities not available to the entire school population, such as foreign-language instruction, field trips, or courses focused on poetry writing or journalism. At the secondary level, the focus may be on career awareness and planning that culminates in field experience and working with a mentor (Middlebrooks & Strong, 1982). On the other hand, some enrichment programs can be used equally effectively with nongifted students. Interdisciplinary courses, for example, tying literature to social studies, with perhaps a dollop of fine arts added, can be a much richer experience for *all* students in the upper middle or secondary school. A fine example, and one that could be effectively modified for less gifted eighth graders, is a program designed to correlate the English and social studies curricula at the Hunter College Campus Schools (Warner & Rosof, 1992).

Enrichment programs typically mean that the gifted students are taken out of their regular classes, more often at the elementary school level than the secondary, for part or all of a day to work with a resource teacher. The fact that they leave the classroom (as do other students for other purposes) is a principal disadvantage to this option. Not only does this differentiate the gifted from the nongifted children, but they often miss instruction that is important for them to have; and it is not always easy for the classroom teacher to reteach the material or to give a test a second time because of time constraints and the needs of others in the class. As a result, as R. M. Milgram and Goldring (1991) pointed out, the regular teacher "often views the pull-out program as disruptive and thus may be antagonistic towards the gifted child" (p. 30).

In addition, pullout classes may not be viable because there are too few children to make them practical as an alternative or they may be too expensive simply because of the added teaching staff, materials, and space needed for them. Despite these negative aspects, nevertheless, there are situations where enrichment classes may be the only feasible option available, even if presented in a nontraditional format (e.g., an extremely gifted 8-year-old in a rural area who is academically on a sixth- or seventh-grade level and can profit from intensely accelerated instruction in mathematics, science, or foreign language may have such instruction via television).

Homogeneous Classes

Subsumed under the heading of homogeneous are not only classes and academic tracks for the academically gifted, but also selective schools. In the past, some of these schools have been sex segregated, but in recent years most of them have admitted both girls and boys.

Like all programs for gifted students, the existence of such homogeneous classes and schools has long stirred controversy about elitism and the pressure such situations place on the gifted and talented youth. Although Marsh (1991) and others have suggested that it may be more beneficial to be a "big fish in a little pond"—what he calls the big-fish-little-pond effect (BFLPE)—other writers and some of the graduates themselves support the idea of a more homogeneous student body as providing more challenge, more peers like oneself, and less boredom. As has been noted elsewhere in this section, it can be a shock of sorts when gifted students first encounter others like themselves and are no longer the outstanding student in a class, grade, or school. The frame of reference, or size of the pond, has changed. Marsh's finding, based on a largely statistical analysis of 23 factors, is that attendance at a selective high school has negative effects on the academically able as seen in their sophomore and senior years, and even in college.

> On average, equally able students attending higher-ability high schools were likely to select less demanding coursework and to have lower academic self-concepts, lower GPAs, lower educational aspirations, and lower occupational aspirations in both their sophomore and senior years of high school. The negative effects of attending higher-ability schools were also shown for scores on 72 ability tests and college attendance, although these effects were very small. (p. 470)

He admits that the negative effects during high school were small and were based on averages across 1,000 high schools and "many thousands" of students (p. 476). Nevertheless, his study provides food for thought and caution. (My own question would be what coursework at a selective high school Marsh found "less demanding." Was it music, art, home economics, or modern literature instead of classical literature?)

Homogeneous classes refer to those classes in which the abilities of the students are more similar than is true in the regular (mainstream or heterogeneous) class. They may be limited to the upper levels of certain subjects, such as calculus or advanced physics; spread more broadly across an academic track where students are grouped for all subjects with peers of presumably similar ability; or be housed in a special school designed for students of a particular academic level. Academic tracking has its proponents, as does each of the options discussed in these pages, but it has even more vociferous opponents. The core proposition of the opposition is that "rather than merely responding to pre-existing student abilities and needs, tracking shapes and limits students, often along racial and social class lines" ("Teaching inequality," 1989, pp. 1319-1320). Unfortunately, this is too often true. Tracking also may lead to self-fulfilling prophecies and "steadily increasing inequalities" (p. 1333) as teachers expect and demand less of lower tracked students than those in higher tracks. According to research summarized by editors of the *Harvard Education Letter*, "Being in the top track appears to accelerate achievement and being in the low track to reduce it" ("The tracking wars," 1992, p. 2). In addition, it should be noted that across-the-board tracking also fails to take into consideration intraindividual differences with respect to different subject matter.

Homogeneous classes can meet the needs of all students, not only the gifted and talented, if handled in a sensitive and appropriate manner. To reduce the charge of elitism, for example, such classes could be open to students whose IQ is lower than 130 but who have a strong interest in the content *and* who are willing to work to meet the challenge posed by the course. Who knows? They may be among the potentially able, with their abilities belatedly identified because they have been stimulated in a different way. (It should go without saying that their "nongifted" status should not be on the class roll, for teachers need only know that the students in the class are there because they want to be.)

Entire schools and self-sufficient units within schools devoted to the gifted and talented tend to arouse even more opposition than homogeneous classes. Are they different in concept, however, from vocational high schools that specialize in aviation trades, food technology, or commerce and industry? In each case, the students in such special programs have chosen to be there, and where the demand is greater than the number of spaces available, screening and selection occur. It should be made very clear that the demands of such schools or programs are different from, and often greater than, traditional school curricula.

Braddock and McPartland (1993), in the process of advocating *hetero*geneous classes, especially for early adolescents, spell out very clearly some of the problems such classes may have:

Student motivation can suffer when earning high grades is too easy for those at the top of the distribution and too hard for those at the bottom. Teacher effectiveness can decline when classroom materials for a whole group lesson are poorly matched to the prior preparation of various students (e.g., reading matter that is geared to a single grade level when student reading skills range over several grade levels). The classroom climate can also be weakened in a very heterogeneous class when discipline problems arise with students who cannot earn status through academic accomplishment. (p. 147)

Alternatives to tracking, however, do have their advocates. Steinberg and Wheelock (1992) describe two middle school programs that are designed to eliminate the lowest levels of instruction and to establish a climate of high expectations for *all* students. Recognizing the difficulties that some students may have even in such a supportive atmosphere, however, provision is made for them to have extra tutoring or preparation for a new unit of study. (Note that awareness of this extra help may still create self-esteem and peer problems, even with the voiced high expectations for all students.)

An example of a whole school for the gifted, the Hunter College Elementary School was founded as a free model school in 1870 by Thomas Hunter, who also founded what would become known as Hunter College (Stone, 1992). The purpose of the elementary school was to serve as a laboratory for teachers being trained at the higher institution. Even in its early years it provided an uncommon curriculum that included French, German, and music for its young female students. It became a school for gifted youngsters in 1941, admitting children with the highest IQ scores first and working downward to fill the available spaces. "In 1941, the median IQ was at about 120; by 1945 it was up to 151" (Stone, 1992, p. 27). The high school, descended from Hunter's original institution and intended to be a college preparatory school for girls, became a formal entity in 1903 and had entrance exams from the start. Both schools were populated by predominantly middle- and upper-middle-class students, mostly white, and of course, only girls in the high school until 1974 (p. 73). This is a costly option in most settings, but may be feasible if established, as Hunter was, as a college laboratory school (although this does not give teachers in training the experience with varied kinds of students they would find in the larger public school district).

Magnet Schools

In districts with a sufficiently large school population, it may be possible to develop magnet schools, that is, schools with a highly specialized curriculum that draws students interested and able in specific learning areas. They tend to be rigorously academic even when not focused on purely academic subjects. Admission is by examination, portfolio, or audition. The latter two means have long been the practice of schools like the LaGuardia High School of Music and Art in New York and other high schools of performing arts. At some high schools for performing arts, the academic schedule often has to be worked around Wednesday matinee performances or concert tours, as the students are already actively involved in their careers.

The magnet school differs from the more general school for the gifted, like Central High School and the Philadelphia High School for Girls in Philadelphia or the Bronx High School of Science in New York, in that it specializes in a particular field and may include students not identified as gifted. The New York City Board of Education announced in April 1993 the opening of more than three dozen magnet high schools, including one for gifted students. Each school is to be organized around a theme, often vocation or profession oriented, such as health fields, foreign languages, science skills, or leadership and public service (Dillon, 1993). Some magnet schools are even found at the elementary level, like the Masterman School in Philadelphia or the Trotter Elementary School in Boston. According to one source, "Magnets gained popularity as an alternative to mandatory busing" as a means of desegregating schools (Toch, Linnon, & Cooper, 1991, p. 61).

In many cases, magnet schools are located adjacent to resource facilities related to the school's focus, such as a zoo, a university, an aerospace company, or a museum. Applications tend to outnumber places available, so some screening is necessary, with admission more often offered to those "most likely to succeed" in the program because of a combination of interest and ability. "Educators suspect . . . that the very act of selecting a school contributes powerfully to a student's performance there" (Toch et al., 1991, p. 62), although there is little hard evidence of this available to date. When housed within a larger school, magnet school supporters suggest that they may stimulate greater effort toward achievement on the part of nonmagnet students as well.

In the case of Montgomery Blair High School in Silver Spring, Maryland, selection of students for the research-oriented math and science curriculum is "based on grades, standardized test scores, and the completion of algebra by the eighth grade" ("In a minority district," 1993, p. B13). (This program was designed to desegregate the school, located in a largely black and Hispanic district, by attracting more white and Asian students to the school, which it has done; but fewer than 15% of those in the program are black and Hispanic, a major concern of local school officials.) That the school is successful academically is apparent in the fact that it had three students among the top 40 finalists in the 1993 Westinghouse Science Talent Search, and all three placed in the top 10 winners ("Chicago student wins," 1993, p. A17).

Again, this is a costly alternative and one that can be managed best, perhaps, in a large city. However, there is no real reason why a sizable suburban school or a large consolidated school cannot create "schools within schools" to achieve the same "magnet" effect. Indeed, there is currently movement in this direction to reduce the anonymity too many students feel in large schools; tailoring the curriculum to interests or abilities could be made part of the planning and restructuring.

Acceleration

There are variations in the ways in which acceleration can be used with gifted and talented students,

> but all are based on the assumption that gifted students will learn more in less time than is allowed for the instruction of students in the general program.... By *acceleration* we mean raising the level and/or pace of instruction to be commensurate with students' achievement levels and capacity or rate of learning. (Feldhusen, 1991, p. 133)

One mode of acceleration is to allow the gifted student to take one or two courses above his or her normal high school grade placement. Such subject matter acceleration can also be done at the elementary school level if there is departmentalization and careful scheduling.

At the secondary level, especially in a fairly sizable high school, it may be practical for the gifted student to participate in most classes with his/her agemates but move into more advanced courses in one or two subjects of greatest strength (e.g., Algebra II instead of Algebra I in Grade 9, or Advanced French instead of the introductory course). Advanced Placement (AP) courses, which may result in college credit, are another possibility offered at most sizable high schools. This is essentially a form of acceleration, but in subject matter rather than grade level. Such an adjustment in scheduling recognizes that even the academically gifted do not necessarily have the same level of ability in all areas. It does require more administrative effort for scheduling, but if school personnel sincerely mean what they say about meeting the needs of each student, that is a small price to pay.

Another mode is to move the student ahead a full grade or more in all subjects (grade acceleration). Related approaches include early admission to school (age 5 to first grade, for example) and early admission to college, as in the Johns Hopkins program and others to be discussed. Indeed, early admission to school or acceleration in grade or subjects is seen as preventive of *under*achievement in some gifted children or a means of reversing underachievement that has already occurred (Rimm & Lovance, 1992). As might be imagined, there is much opposition to grade acceleration as well as to the other methods on the grounds that children should be kept with their age peers, no matter the cost to the child.

A few decades ago, the New York City schools and others regularly practiced grade acceleration of the academically able, with the result that the students might graduate from high school at age 15 or 16 rather than the more usual age 18. The goal was not necessarily early graduation, but rather trying to keep these students with their peers in level of cognitive development. When semiannual promotion was practiced, students might be advanced by a half grade at a time or placed in a junior high school program that collapsed a 3-year curriculum to 2 or 2½ years (similar to today's curriculum compacting). Since the abandonment of semiannual promotion, this option has been used less frequently, usually on the grounds that skipping the child over a whole grade might be inappropriate for social maturity or physical development and thus more injurious than risking normal progression through the grades.

Christopherson (1979) gives the following rationale:

> Arguments offered to support enrichment and separate programs usually reflect a conception of gifted children as being *different* from other children. If we were to emphasize that gifted children are *like* other children, then we could explore the potential of educating gifted children the way we educate other children. The key is understanding that *gifted children are like older* children. (pp. 1-2)

He postulates that advanced placement according to intellectual level and academic achievement should have an underlying criterion that "the child's level of *intellectual development* should exceed the 80th percentile for the older children" or if in one subject area only, "the child should exceed the 70th percentile for the older children's *achievement* in that subject area" (p. 3). Other possible criteria for related situations are also offered as examples. Christopherson does not think that social, emotional, and physical development should merit major consideration in such acceleration, but that criteria in these areas "should be set only high enough to insure that the child will not be at a special disadvantage in trying to fit in non-academically with the older children" (p. 4). This model reflects both the Terman group's findings that gifted children tend to be physically well developed and other research that indicates that individuals, even if well endowed intellectually in general, typically vary in specific strengths (see Chapter 8). Although Christopherson acknowledges that developmental placement is not the perfect solution to the education of gifted students, it eliminates, in his thinking, the need for specialized enrichment programs or specially trained teachers and thus the expense of special programming. From the taxpayers' point of view, this then becomes an attractive proposal.

If the old semiannual acceleration policy and Christopherson's developmental placement represent gradual acceleration, there are a handful of programs that represent more radical acceleration: the Study of Mathematically Precocious Youth (SMPY) program at Johns Hopkins University, the Texas Academy of Mathematics and Science (TAMS) at the University of North Texas, the Clarkson School of Clarkson University, the Program for the Exceptionally Gifted at Mary Baldwin College, programs at the Gifted Education Resource Institute of Purdue University, the Simon's Rock-Bard College program, and the Early Entrance Program (EEP) at the University of Washington.

In the SMPY Johns Hopkins program, many of those seventh graders identified on the Scholastic Aptitude Test as "intellectually precocious" have been encouraged to accelerate their education not only by participating in advanced math courses for college credit, but in some cases by moving directly from their present placement to college entrance—truly a radical and rapid acceleration. In the North Texas TAMS program, the gifted students "live on campus, take college courses, and complete the last two years of high school and the first two years of college concurrently" (Lupkowski, Whitmore, & Ramsay, 1992, p. 88).

Part of the rationale for a radical approach is that "acceleration should enhance gifted students' achievement motivation" (Richardson

& Benbow, 1990, p. 464). Another consideration is that both their short- and long-term academic performance benefit. In what Feldhusen (1983) terms *integrative acceleration*, the essence of the program involves challenge as well as rapid, compressed content; a wide range of topics; and advanced levels of material along with more of it. Critics of this approach express concern about the effects of radical acceleration on the youths' social and emotional development.

Richardson and Benbow (1990) surveyed more than 1,200 accelerated youths who had participated in the first three SMPY talent searches in the early 1970s (age 18, after high school; age 23, after college) using a self-report questionnaire that covered self-esteem, locus of control, social interaction, and self-acceptance/identity. The latter two items included the following note: "Indicate the degree to which your total acceleration (kindergarten to present) has affected you overall in each of the following areas" (p. 470). Overall, Richardson and Benbow did not find support for fears about social or emotional maladjustment resulting from rapid acceleration, although a very weak negative correlation was found between grade acceleration and self-esteem ($r = -.09$) and also for participation in segregated (e.g., enrichment) programs for gifted students (p. 468).

An earlier study by Pollins (1983) with radical accelerants in the SMPY group had found "no negative effects of acceleration on social and emotional development. In fact, some evidence of positive effect" was found (p. 176). Citing both their own research and that of Festinger (1954), Richardson and Benbow (1990) concluded that "being placed in a higher grade with older students or in segregated classes for the gifted may result in gifted students' comparing themselves with other gifted or advanced students. Self-concepts are predicted to decline in such instances" (p. 468). Further, any negative effects on social and emotional development, according to these researchers, may result not from the acceleration per se but from the extreme intellectual abilities of the individuals or from age. "Less than 3.5% of the accelerated students reported at age 23 negative effects on self-acceptance/identity or on their social interactions" (p. 468).

Another study, also concerned with the impact of early entrance to college on self-esteem, surveyed gifted students in the TAMS program. These 14- to 17-year-olds completed the Adult form of the Coopersmith Self-Esteem Inventory during their first week in the accelerated program ($N = 185$) and again after their first semester ($N = 113$). There were no gender differences in either the presemester or postsemester scores, and the observed statistically significant (but relatively slight) drop in self-esteem scores was deemed to have "little practical significance" (Lupkowski et al., 1992, p. 89). Some of the change was related to family relations, which is typical for many college students away from home for the first time, and some, as Richardson and Benbow (1990) had also indicated, was related to the new situation of being only one gifted person among many rather than being unique as in the home school.

The Coopersmith Inventory was employed in another small study, this time with extremely intelligent youngsters (IQ 160-200) in Australia. These were children who had taught themselves to read, write, and count by age 2 or 3. Gross (1992) reports not only their unusual competencies and test scores, but also the barriers and opportunities that have confronted them in their schools, or as she put it, "educational mismanagement" (p. 96). Of the 40 extremely gifted subjects studied by Gross, 9 were radically accelerated.

> It might be anticipated that exceptionally gifted children who have been radically accelerated would score highly on the index of academic self-esteem. By contrast, they display positive but modest scores, between the mean for their age groups and .7 of a standard deviation above. These students compare their academic performance with that of their classmates who are several years their senior. They still outperform their classmates and they enjoy the intellectual and academic challenge, but they have to work to achieve their success. (p. 97)

On the other hand, those subjects who were not radically accelerated have markedly inflated scores on academic self-esteem, but very negative perceptions of their social skills and images in the eyes of their peers. Most experienced great difficulty in developing positive social relationships with their classmates, which was not true of the radically accelerated group (p. 97).

In a study focused on the EEP at the University of Washington, Janos, Sanfilippo, and Robinson (1986) tried to find out what differentiated participants ($N = 12/56$) who were underachieving (GPA $\leq$ 2.9) from those who were earning GPAs of 3.0 or greater ($N = 44/56$). They describe the underachievers as

> earning significantly lower grades than EEP students whose college readiness scores were no higher, and they were self-critical about it. In general, they lacked enthusiasm for their studies. The males, in particular, often lounged lethargically, and sincerely confessed to being bored and depressed. The underachieving females were, on the other hand, typically vitalized by nonacademic activities. (p. 305)

These were undergraduates (and 20 graduates) of the University of Washington who had entered the EEP at about age 14 and who were 16 to 17 years old at the time of the study. It should be noted that the EEP provided transition counseling for these youths who had bypassed high school.

Apart from the usual psychological inventories the subjects completed, their transcripts were examined for clues to the differences in performance. "Most striking about the quarterly grades earned by students with GPAs under 3.0 was their erratic character. These students tended, as a group, to alternate between successful and dismal quarters" (p. 308). They also withdrew from or received "incomplete" for more courses than their achieving peers.

Particularly interesting were the sex differences found in this group. "Lower grades seemed to attend students, particularly males, who were more adolescent than academic, and females with absorbing extracurricular commitments" (p. 310). One of the conclusions drawn from this and related findings was that "admissions procedures for accelerants should probably emphasize readiness for intense and sustained concentration" so as to reduce the possibility of mediocre college records limiting later options for these students (p. 311). This conclusion is supported by other studies. Brody, Assouline, and Stanley (1990), for example, concluded from their study of early entrants at Johns Hopkins that these youths were more likely to be successful in college if they had taken a variety of Advanced Placement courses while in high school and had SAT scores equal to or greater than those of more typical entering freshmen.

Jones and Southern (1991) found three compelling reasons—economy, inevitability, and honesty—for school districts to use acceleration modes for the gifted and talented. Economy concerns both time and school personnel: Teachers have too little time to devote to just a few "deviant" students who need special attention, and there are too few teachers with the training and skill to provide optimal assistance to these students. "As for inevitability, it is nearly impossible to design an intervention that simultaneously challenges all students and avoids any accelerative implications" (p. 226). That is, students who are working at an advanced level, either independently or within the classroom, eventually will need some kind of systematic instruction to help them go further, whether in a foreign language or in mathematics.

Honesty refers to schools' self-proclaimed goal of serving all their students, which is not done if gifted students are obliged to follow a curriculum or use materials that do not suit their intellectual abilities and needs. However, this means that schools must plan carefully what options are available and to determine that these do not penalize the gifted student in terms of college admission or scholarships. For example:

> Schools should ensure that the accelerative options open doors for the student. College credit courses that eliminate a student from honors tracks, or advanced courses that bring a student to a dead end in terms of more advanced work at the high school level, close rather than open opportunities. (p. 227)

Further, these authors caution that the student and his or her parents must want the acceleration. (At a Johns Hopkins meeting in the mid-1970s, for example, one student who qualified for early admission to college said that she preferred to take college courses as an "extra" because she had certain extracurricular activities through her high school that she wished to continue with her peers.)

Most studies indicate that acceleration, in whatever form, has positive academic outcomes for the gifted student. There are fewer studies, however, that focus on the social and psychological outcomes, making it difficult to support a general positive or negative view of consequences in these areas (K. B. Rogers & Kimpston, 1992). Most of the subjects in the University of Washington EEP who were asked about their reaction to skipping high school had positive reactions, except for the obvious problems associated with being too young to drive even though they were college students (Noble & Drummond, 1992).

A second group of students who found radical acceleration to be a positive solution to the many negatives they have encountered as extremely gifted students (IQ ≥160) were the 40 Australian youngsters mentioned above. "In every case," wrote Gross (1992),

> the students who have been radically accelerated, and their teachers and parents, believe strongly that they are now much more appropriately placed, both academically and socially.... They have a greater number of friends and enjoy closer and more productive social relationships than they did prior to their acceleration. They have significantly higher levels of social and general self-esteem than do children of equal intellectual ability who have been retained with age-peers or grade-skipped by a single year. (p. 98)

It should go without saying that their advancement was both carefully planned and carefully monitored, which is neither more nor less than is demanded in the education of all exceptional children.

Mentoring

Mentors exist in the corporate world, in the military world, in some areas of academia, and to a lesser extent, in the educational world below the graduate school level. In graduate school, the professor-adviser often co-authors papers, sponsors conference attendance, and writes letters of recommendation for a promising graduate student, thus getting the student off to a good start in an academic career. A senior professor, for example, who introduces new colleagues to the intricacies of a campus's bureaucracy, offers suggestions for improving course presentations, and guides them in the tenure and promotion process, is serving as a mentor. Similarly, an experienced attorney may take a new associate around City Hall to introduce the associate to people with whom he or she will have to work to obtain needed legal documents or to schedule hearings. Taking a new colleague under one's wing is both a service and a responsibility, for the mentor must be both an appropriate model and a "giver" rather than a "taker." Such activity is usually associated with working with young adults, however, rather than with adolescents or younger children.

Participation in a mentoring program has a number of advantages for the gifted youth, including gaining a realistic view of the work world generally and specific careers. The knowledge and skills that can be acquired and applied in another field if goals change, "are of three types: (a) knowledge of how successful professionals interact effectively, (b) skills specific to the career field, and (c) thinking skills which can be generalized" (Edlind & Haensley, 1985, p. 57). For the mentor, there is personal satisfaction at seeing a newcomer become acquainted with and excited by her or his field of interest as well as fulfillment of the responsibility to prepare the next generation to play its role in a field.

One aspect of Kaufmann's (1981) study of the 1964-1968 Presidential Scholars dealt with the role of mentors. Of the 139 subjects responding to questions about mentors, about two thirds reported that their most significant mentors had been teachers, almost half in graduate school and 29% in secondary school. "The functions of the mentor that were most frequently described were role modeling (61%), support and encouragement (58%), and professional socialization (13%)... . The gifted participants perceived that role modeling and support and encouragement were the most important functions their mentor served" (Kaufmann, Harrel, Milam, Woolverton, & Miller, 1986, p. 577). More than half of the mentorships lasted 1 to 3 years, with 57% of the respondents claiming that they had adopted some of their mentor's habits and attitudes.

Kaufmann et al. (1986) suggest that school counselors can play significant roles in helping to develop mentoring relationships:

1. Providing information to potential mentors and mentees about the advantages of mentoring
2. Assisting in the identification and matching of individuals on the bases of interests, values, and teaching-learning styles
3. Establishing and monitoring mentorship programs in schools or professional organizations
4. Providing ongoing training in mentoring
5. Providing support groups for participants in mentoring relationships (p. 577)

Kornhaber et al. (1990) advocate mentoring and apprenticeships as means of "enabling" intelligences, giving the mentee the opportunity to work closely "with the central issues and materials of a field" and to "embed learning in a social and purposeful context" that builds on student interests and strengths and also fosters "critical thinking through regular, informal assessment in the context of an authentic domain" (p. 191). These advantages, of course, are not limited to the gifted in any field, but, they assert, should be offered to all children and youth.

In the CHALLENGE program in one school district, a mentoring program proved to be the key to motivating gifted middle school students (Booth, 1980). Mentors were recruited from the community, and the seventh and eighth graders worked one half day every other week with them. Selection of each apprenticeship involved the student, the parents, and the mentor. As has been noted previously, working with middle school students is particularly important, because this may be the last real chance to "turn them on" to school and to long-term goals. The mentor-apprenticeship format provides a glimpse of what the end result of years in school can be in content of work involved and potential income (usually a good motivator) and so is especially valuable for this age group.

As suggested in the examples given, there should be some frequency of contact between the mentor and the mentee over a period of time, whether face to face, as is preferable, or by more indirect means. The frequency and nature of the contacts should be agreed upon before the relationship begins. One potential difficulty has been raised in articles dealing with mentors for females (e.g., Bogat & Redner, 1985): There are too few female mentors available. Some programs, however, like Math Options discussed earlier, are making specific efforts to overcome this problem.

Mentoring is the option that potentially costs the district least in dollars with the possibility of the greatest rewards for the participants. In addition, the sources of mentors range from colleagues to retirees to the business and professional community. In fact, gifted secondary school students might find it exciting and rewarding to serve as mentors to younger gifted students. It is certainly appropriate to offer mentors a stipend, expense reimbursement, or an honorarium, but most will turn these offers down. Their reward is the bubbling enthusiasm or growth of the young person with whom they've been working. Indeed, they may even gain a different or refreshed perspective of their field for themselves.

Independent Study

Independent study can mean many things: self-set explorations, one-on-one formal instruction with a teacher or tutor outside of the school system, or correspondence courses.

As an example of the first type, suppose that a youngster has read a novel by Theodore Dreiser and become fascinated with his style or the times about which he wrote. She proceeds to locate and read everything else he wrote and then seeks out biographical data on Dreiser, with the goal of writing a definitive essay on the author and his work.

In the second form of independent study, a verbally talented child takes weekly lessons in Sanskrit from a local professor simply out of desire to learn the language and later to read works written in Sanskrit. One can even visualize a gifted prospective attorney, age 11 or 12 years, eagerly doing research in a law office in a modern-day version of the on-site training prospective lawyers had a century ago.

Correspondence study, the third form of independent study, has a tie with distance education in that it serves students in rural as well as well-populated areas. The content can be almost anything from photography to Latin. Indeed, Latin is one of the subjects offered in Duke University's By-Mail Program for gifted middle school students (Sawyer, DeLong, & von Brock, 1987). The program was designed by the Talent Identification Program primarily to serve gifted rural youngsters who would otherwise not have access to advanced courses in mathematics or foreign language, or who were deemed ineligible for existing high school courses by virtue of their grade level. Students in this program are supplied with a high-level textbook and other materials, and are assigned a mentor either at Duke or in their locality.

Several of the courses in Duke's program lead to the Advanced Placement (AP) examination, including American History, Latin, Calculus, English Language and Composition, English Literature and Composition, Biology, Chemistry, and two areas in Physics. In 1982-1985, of 61 students who took AP exams in these fields, 26 (43%) earned a score of 5 (the highest level), 15 earned a 4, 19 earned a 3, and one earned a 2 (Sawyer et al., 1987, p. 119). These scores compared very favorably with the national average where "35 percent received a grade of '4' or higher; and 14 percent received a grade of '5'" (p. 120), especially when one considers that the correspondence students had an average age of 15 years, 7 months. German and Russian are also offered by correspondence, but students have first to successfully complete a summer residential program at Duke.

Yet another form of independent study, not necessarily purely academic, is using computer software. Where the family can afford to purchase a computer, and these are becoming less expensive every year, even the preschool gifted youngster can use this technology for independent learning at his or her own pace. Educational software not only teaches reading and mathematical skills, but provides interactive simulation and decision-making games that enhance the child's abilities to solve problems and to anticipate possible outcomes. Other software programs offer foreign-language instruction (complete with sound), geography and map making, music theory and composition, mechanical or freehand drawing, puzzle construction, and scientific or engineering concepts. The gifted child who is a potential author will find the word processing function of a computer a definite aid to writing, with the drudgery of revision (i.e., retyping or rewriting in longhand) reduced tremendously. The spelling check and dictionary aspects of some word processing programs also enhance writing.

Independent study rarely costs the school district more than making space available for catalogs of correspondence courses and educational software, which are themselves cost free. It would help the gifted child and his/her family, of course, if a counselor had enough knowledge about the programs to provide appropriate guidance, again, cost free to the district.

Distance Education

"Distance education" refers to instruction conveyed via television; a combination of videotapes, conference telephone, and on-site teacher's aide; or computers with modems in locations where there are typically too few students to warrant the expense of hiring a teacher on site or even to commute once a week perhaps hundreds of miles. Distance education has been used to provide science, advanced mathematics, and other courses to schools in relatively isolated areas or with very small enrollments. As an example, "1990-91 offerings of the Satellite Educational Resources Consortium (SERC) to schools in a 23-state network included an honors section on world geography; advanced placement sections in economics, physics, and mathematics; and sections of Russian and Japanese" (Howard, Ault, Knowlton, & Swall, 1992, p. 276).

Distance education has also been employed extensively for adult college and graduate education, with lectures transmitted in the early morning hours on weekends or in the evening to widely dispersed students. As technology makes it possible, interactive television (ITV) will permit teacher and students at different sites not only to have verbal interaction, but also to be able to see each other, much as in a traditional classroom (Howard et al., 1992).

As for cost, there is certainly an initial outlay for the necessary television equipment and satellite dish as well as a license fee for using a program. Typically, however, the licensing fees are very small compared to the salaries for specialist teachers, and the costs of the equipment can be amortized over several years.

Summer, Weekend, and Other Special Programs

The number of "extracurricular" programs for gifted and other students appears to be growing at a rapid rate, with new ones being opened annually. Many of the programs are relatively short term, 2 to 4 weeks, for example, but intensive because they are residential. Other programs are offered on weekends throughout the year or after regular school hours and are attended on a commuting basis.

Given the need of the mathematically gifted for an atypical curriculum and the difficulty this seems to pose for most school systems, alternative opportunities need to be developed (Heid, 1983). One such example is a summer program that has been offered by the Maryland Department of Education. It provides the unique kinds of problems that the mathematically gifted student finds especially stimulating, challenging, and pleasurable.

For gifted young students who live too far from the University of Maryland or Johns Hopkins to participate in their special programs, especially those that proceed through traditional mathematics in an accelerated mode, weekend classes in their community provide the opportunity to move along as quickly as they're able. For some youths, college credit is earned, giving them an accelerated start when they enter a college or university.

Another program designed by the Center for the Advancement of Academically Talented Youth at Johns Hopkins combines weekend classes and a summer residential program. This is the Skills Reinforcement Project (SRP), which is intended to reinforce basic skills and develop higher level thinking skills of potentially gifted middle and junior high school minority youth (Lynch & Mills, 1990). In addition to the academic aspects, the program helps these children to learn the behaviors important for success, including study skills and attention to detail, and to develop a positive self-image, self-confidence, and other related affective characteristics.

A summer Discovery program at the University of Pennsylvania in 1992 offered workshops to aspiring young writers, camping and field trips related to biology, and courses as diverse as Creating and Producing a Radio Program for Grades 4-6, Introduction to the Stock Market for Grades 7-10, and Issues in Bioethics and Science for Grades 10-12. Many of these courses were taught by college professors or teachers of the gifted and certainly went beyond traditional curriculum for these youngsters.

Pennsylvania has five Governor's Schools of Excellence, which are 5-week residential summer programs. These are open to 10th- and 11th-grade students who are highly able or talented in the arts, sciences, or agricultural sciences or who have abilities and interests directing them toward teaching or health care. Graduates of one of these Governor's schools are eligible for college scholarships offered by several of the commonwealth's public and private higher education institutions.

Another residential program, this one designed for academically talented students in Grades 4-11, is the New Jersey-based Summer Institute for the Gifted. For 3 weeks, 800-900 identified gifted and talented students from across the United States and abroad live, study, and play at one of two college preparatory schools or at Bryn Mawr College or Vassar College. College credit courses are offered for high school students, who can take an examination given by and receive a college transcript from the Thomas Edison State College. Courses offered in 1993 for students in Grades 4-6 included Problem Solving Analysis, Exploring the Universe, Creative Writing, An Introduction to Mock Trials, and Laboratory Experiments in Chemistry; for Grades 6-8 there were several mathematics courses, Robotics and Microelectronics, Journalism, Introduction to Veterinary Medicine, Public Speaking, Introduction to Psychology, and Archaeology; for Grades 8-11 courses included Experiments in Physics, the Art of Debate,

College Chemistry, and Pascal Programming. In addition, cultural courses in theater arts, dance, photography, and other fields were offered, and a variety of recreational courses from golf to team sports to chess were available to these students.

Western Carolina University offers 2- and 4-week summer residential programs to gifted students in Grades 5-10. The Cullowhee Experience combines a challenging curriculum, including even the opportunity for individual research programs, with the usual recreational and cultural activities associated with a good summer camp.

Some summer programs are clearly career oriented, although not always limited to the identified gifted and talented. One is the 1993 Yale Summer Psychology Program designed by Robert J. Sternberg, and open to 9th to 11th graders screened for strength in traditional analytic intelligence, creative intelligence, or practical intelligence. Another is the National Law Camp, aimed at high school and college students, many or most of whom are considered "brains." The U.S. Space and Rocket Center houses a space camp; medical groups sponsor camps; talented music students spend their summers at Interlochen, Michigan; and a growing number of professional organizations are similarly hosting special programs.

Does the experience in weekend or summer programs do anything for the gifted besides teach them? According to a study by Kolloff and Moore (1989) that involved more than 500 gifted students in Grades 5-10, there was almost universal gain in self-concept. Part of the gain was attributed to the fact that the youngsters were part of a group in which they did not have to hide their abilities and part to the spirit and friendships that arise in a residential program. Children with musical gifts or dramatic talents and above-average academic ability are frequently identified early by their parents (with some confirmation of their appraisal by a professional) and frequently have few peers with whom to share their abilities and interests. For these young children, summer programs for similarly gifted agemates are stimulating. Similarly, secondary school students with artistic and academic talent in a 2-week summer program who found their regular teachers to be nonchallenging, nonsupportive of accomplishment, or noninstructive in new techniques welcomed the opportunity to be with others like themselves (Clark & Zimmerman, 1988).

The cost of these weekend and summer programs varies but is often several hundred to a few thousand dollars for a residential 4-week program. Typically, the cost is borne by the family, but in some cases scholarships are provided for state-run programs or by sponsoring foundations or institutions.

Conclusion

In looking at these various options, it is apparent that there are many ways in which gifted and talented students may be helped to enhance their school experiences without sacrificing social or emotional adjustment. Although recognizing that both replacement and supplementary programs can be helpful to gifted and talented youths, R. M. Milgram (1992) also indicates the varied disadvantages that they have. I believe she would agree, however, with Feldhusen's (1991) conclusions following a review of a number of studies of programs for these youth, that the major needs of gifted and talented youth are:

1. Instruction in the basic subject matters at levels and pace that fit their precocity
2. Interaction with peers of like ability
3. Intellectual challenges that develop sound thinking skills. (p. 143)

In many cases, these options can be and are combined. Recommending acceleration should be done on an individual basis and is appropriately seen as one option among many, rather than being adopted as a general school district policy. People working in both basic and higher education can themselves be highly creative in designing programs to meet the needs of gifted and talented youth. With the support of school board members and educational administrators, these programs could help to meet the needs of even more gifted and talented students.

8 Follow-Up Studies

In recent years particularly, there have been a number of studies of adults who were identified as gifted in childhood or adolescence. These studies are important for the clues they can provide to the effects of identification itself, differing patterns of education, and parental and teacher influences.

It is important to keep in mind, however, that the cohorts functioned in different eras; I have attempted to place the studies in a roughly chronological sequence to reflect this. Terman's subjects, for example, matured during the Great Depression of the 1930s, whereas the Johns Hopkins project and others have flourished only in the past two decades. Not only have economic times changed from Depression to post-World War II prosperity to recession beginning in the late 1980s, but social attitudes have changed toward women being in the workforce, technology has advanced at an unbelievable rate, and higher education is assumed to be within almost everyone's reach and to be almost everyone's "right."

Accordingly, what might have seemed remarkable for some gifted children now in their very senior years might be taken for granted among those only now in college. The follow-up studies, which vary in rigor as well as in number of subjects, must be read with these differences in mind.

Terman's Study

The most durable longitudinal study of the gifted, as well as the pioneer effort in this field, is the one begun by Lewis Terman seven decades ago. Despite Terman's personal biases and the many flaws inherent in the original and follow-up phases of the study, all duly elaborated by Shurkin (1992), the fact is that Terman and his students (and their students) have been able to gather information on a large number of subjects ($N = 1{,}444$) from childhood to old age. The original subject sample was seriously nonrepresentative of the population, with significant biases in favor of Caucasian males who were children of professional fathers and families of Northern European/ British origin (Shurkin, 1992, pp. 36-41). This reflects not only Terman's belief in the genetic transmission of intelligence, but also the view that dominated society's thinking at the time (early 1920s). Another reflection of society's thinking can be seen in this passage from Terman's first volume on his study:

> To what extent the sex differences in reading interests reflect differences in native endowment, and to what extent the subtle effects of social ideals and training, it is impossible to say. It is the tradition of our race that men should be interested in such things as industries, machinery, and the sciences, and that woman's sphere is the home. The girl is exposed to this tradition from her earliest years, and it would be surprising if such long-continued and pervading suggestion did not leave its mark on her reading interests. (1925, p. 450)

At the time of follow-up in the 1940s, Terman found that acceleration of his gifted subjects, the typical mode of handling the very able student at that time, had had positive effects on their college and graduate school careers and no negative effects on their physical or mental health (Shurkin, 1992, p. 155). By 1955, he found that almost half of his male subjects (45.6%) were in professional occupations, with an additional 40.7% in semiprofessional and managerial occupations. The increase of 15% in the latter group since the 1940 follow-up doubtless reflected both increased responsibility due to experience and the opportunities provided by the G.I. Bill of 1944, as well as other factors (Shurkin, 1992, p. 214).

By 1960, Terman's successors (Pauline Sears, Robert Sears, and Lee Cronbach) found that the sample had a lower death rate than their age cohorts in the general population, virtually no criminal record, and many accomplishments (3 memberships in the National Academy of Science, 350 patents, 2,500 articles and papers, 200 books and monographs in the sciences and humanities, 2 ambassadorships, and numerous positions of responsibility in the federal government) (Shurkin, 1992, pp. 271-274).

The data are not always as detailed for the female subjects as for the males. Nevertheless, a follow-up of more than 430 of Terman's women after 50 years, when they averaged age 62, "showed a higher percentage employed as compared to full-time homemakers . . . , more of the married women . . . were childless, . . . and far more had better education and more professional levels of employment than did the other [normative] samples" (P. S. Sears & Barbee, 1977, p. 56).

In summarizing the several decades of follow-up, Shurkin found:

> The most successful of the Termites [as Terman's subjects were nicknamed] were people who had the ability to set goals for themselves and the perseverance to achieve them. They were taught by their parents to be independent and to take the initiative. They were instilled with self-confidence. One important fact that stands out is that whatever the attributes that lead to success were, they were in place by the time the Termites got to high school. . . .
>
> One thing their high level of intelligence gave the Termites was armor, both economic and emotional. . . . Intelligence gave them some independence and more choice. . . . Another factor that seems to pop out of the Terman study is the importance of work. The happiest, most satisfied people were the people who were pleased with their work and were good at it, even exceeding family life in its importance in many cases. (Shurkin, 1992, p. 294)

The Termites are now well into their 80s and 90s and are presumably still being followed. Although bias was evident in their selection almost seven decades ago, it is apparent that the combination of supportive family environments and their own intellectual abilities and inner strengths have enabled most members of this gifted sample to weather successfully very turbulent decades in our nation's history.

Hunter High's Girls

Two of the follow-up studies that focused specifically on the differences and similarities among gifted students from different eras are the Walker and Freeland (1986) and Walker, Reis, and Leonard (1992) studies of women who chose to attend a highly selective school for gifted girls (Hunter College High School in New York City) in the decades from the 1910s through the 1980s. (The high school became coeducational in the mid-1970s.) The earlier study sought to "identify variables influencing gifted women's personal development, educational choices, and vocational growth" (Walker & Freeland, 1986, p. 27). An analysis of the 30 responses received delineated benefits and liabilities of their educational experiences and effects of parental and other influences. This research provided some direction for the later study.

The second study was focused on the question: "What impact have the sociocultural expectations affecting various generations had on gifted females during their life spans?" (p. 203). In excess of 500 women responded to a lengthy questionnaire, providing information on their personality characteristics, attitudes and beliefs, and "potential problematic issues resulting from being a gifted female, such as pressure to curtail achievement in order to maintain friendships, lack of female role models, society's expectation, and so forth" (p. 203). (Although there were respondents from both the 1910s and 1980s decades, they were too few in number to include in the data analysis.)

Demographic information revealed that 92% of the sample was college educated, 52% of the college graduates had some postgraduate education, and just under 16% had attained a professional degree (Ph.D., M.D., J.D., or D.D.). These figures reveal commitment and achievement far in excess of the average for female peers over the years. Across the decades, almost three fourths (73%) of these women chose to work outside the home or to combine career and homemaking, and until relatively recently, most of these women were in fields considered traditional for women (e.g., education, social work). This figure, however, is based on 60%-65% working in the 1920s-1950s, 85% in the 1960s, and 95% in the 1970s (Walker et al., 1992, pp. 203-204). Levels of ambition, assertiveness, adventurousness, dependency, and happiness varied both by decade and by career/homemaking status.

There were several concerns held by women across the decades:

> The common concerns include vague and traditional school and societal expectations, lack of challenging curriculum, concerns about or denial of being labeled gifted, and inadequate athletic programs for females. The women in our study also cited lack of role models, little organized mentoring and few networking skills, and "unhelpful, unchallenging, and perfunctory guidance and counseling." (Walker et al., 1992, pp. 205-206)

Although many if not most of the subjects had obviously achieved success, the problems itemized above suggest that some problems do not change regardless of decade and regardless of laws passed to ensure equal rights for all. Thus the gifted in the 1970s may well have had to deal with some of the same doubts about the value of higher (or graduate) education for women as did women who could have been their grandmothers.

The "Quiz Kids"

In the 1940s and early 1950s, Sunday evening radio, and for a short time television, was enlivened by the seemingly (to other kids) omniscient "Quiz Kids," who ranged in age from 4 to 16 years when they participated. It was a controversial program, for many people thought that it was shameful to exploit young children for the benefit of advertisers, whereas others thought that the youngsters were placed under too much pressure.

Ruth Duskin Feldman, one of the Quiz Kids, has recounted the history of the show and the activities of its wunderkinder during and after World War II. She located about 130 of the estimated 600 participants more than 30 years later for a follow-up study (1982)—the primary reason for including mention of the show here. Sixty-nine ex-Quiz Kids responded to her questionnaire, and she was able to interview about a dozen others.

"Touted as prodigies, we bore a refreshing resemblance to the boy or girl next door. Interviewers expecting pale, bespectacled bookworms or overbearing little monsters were surprised to find us 'just kids'" (p. xiv). Some of the Quiz Kids were tormented by their teachers, whereas others expressed great pleasure that girls were included among those recognized as gifted in memory (the primary criterion for being selected). Apart from all the information they had gained from a wide range of reading, most were well informed on current events and several were talented in the arts.

Of Feldman's respondents, 16 had professional degrees, 12 had doctorates, and several had more than one bachelor's or master's degree. Nearly half mentioned membership in honorary academic societies or graduation from college with honors; more than 20 respondents had received scholarships from prestigious universities or grants from government agencies. Comparison with Terman's gifted group, who were born 20 or more years earlier, revealed that the Quiz Kids had outdistanced the Termites in percent of college graduates, percent of doctorates or professional degrees, occupational success, and for the women, juggling family and career (p. 348).

"Only fifteen of the respondents feel their participation in the program directly affected their careers, but in some cases the impact was powerful" (p. 334). By "powerful," they meant that they became even more committed to scholarship or other activities, thus leading to Fulbright scholarships or similar opportunities. In several cases, even one appearance on the show opened the door to a college education or employment and also provided the self-confidence needed to pursue their chosen activities.

One Quiz Kid, James Dewey Watson, was a co-winner of the Nobel Prize in 1962 for the discovery of the structure of DNA; another, Vanessa Brown, became a well-known Hollywood actress; several became educators in basic or higher education; both males and females became doctors and lawyers. All but two of the female respondents married, most had children, and all were employed full-time for most of their adult lives. Many of the grown-up Quiz Kids have opted, however, for self-actualization rather than status seeking, according to their responses (p. 357).

Despite some unpleasant experiences with peers or teachers at the time, "the vast majority feel the experience had a positive overall effect—in some cases, more so than they thought at the time" (p. 338). They not only interacted with others of equal ability, a novelty for many of the Quiz Kids, but also met famous people all over the country, from President Truman to sports and movie figures. A few are quoted as having had "stage fright"; others mention that they suffered from fear of failure when they were on the air. Looking backward, Feldman quotes one respondent as representing the tenor of the group. He said, "I have not been as successful as my wildest dreams, yet I have been more successful than anyone had a right to expect" (p. 343).

In trying to analyze what made these children as gifted as they were, Feldman includes creative ability, adaptiveness, academic aptitude, persistence and commitment, intuitive ability, judgment, versatility, and initiative (pp. 350-355). Supportive, but not domineering, parents were also clearly seen as an asset. The best parents made them feel "special" rather than "different" (p. 359). Respondents to Feldman's questionnaire urged parents of gifted children to encourage, challenge realistically, and offer opportunities to their children, but not to push the children toward goals they themselves do not want.

The Presidential Scholars

Yet another follow-up study is one that looked at gifted youth who were named Presidential Scholars in 1964-1968 (Kaufmann, 1981). They were selected

> from a pool of 14,000 candidates who scored in the top half of 1% on the 1963-1967 National Merit Scholarship Qualify-

ing Test (NMSQT) in their respective states.... Approximately 120 Presidential Scholars (one male and one female from each state), plus 15 scholars at large, were selected annually.... A total of 604 individuals comprised the 1964-1968 Presidential Scholars. (p. 165)

Kaufmann was able to locate 83% of this population and received responses to a questionnaire she sent them from 64% (or 53% of the total group). Of these, 47% were female and 53% were male, and 97% of them had earned college degrees. More than half of the respondents (61%) had already earned graduate degrees, and an additional 22% were enrolled in graduate school at the time of the follow-up study. Eighty-nine percent of the subjects earned honors in college, with about 10% of them receiving 10 or more awards in college and about 23% receiving awards or special recognition in their careers outside of school.

At the time of the follow-up study, the respondents were in their late 20s and early 30s. Their post-high school lives, both college and career, occurred during a period of national turbulence over civil rights and the Vietnam War. Nevertheless, most of them appeared to be fulfilling their promise as gifted students.

As for occupational classification and status, a majority of subjects chose professions that reflected a high level of

> education and intellectual ability [college professor, physician, lawyer]. Further, the types of adult achievement most frequently reported (e.g., publications, presentations at professional meetings, research grants, staff training, and having their suggestions adopted by colleagues) reflect the subjects' persistence in striving for excellence and recognition in job-related endeavors. (p. 167)

Kaufmann did find that there were gender differences in types of jobs held and in income. Given the time frame, mostly the 1970s, she hypothesized that these might be due to the at that time still-prevalent inequalities of opportunity, sex role expectations, and possibly the "motive to avoid success" postulated by Horner (1970). (Some of the females reported, however, that they had been helped by the incipient women's movement.)

Study of Mathematically Precocious Youth (SMPY)

Another group of gifted youth who have been studied over an extended period of years includes those who have participated in the

Study of Mathematically Precocious Youth (SMPY) at Johns Hopkins University. Many of the students had scores on SATs and other measures that were so high when they were in seventh grade that they were invited to enter college on a radically accelerated schedule. Others attended weekend mathematics workshops that enabled them to acquire college credits while still in high school and thus enter college with advanced standing.

Although the information about these students is longitudinal in nature rather than retrospective as for some of the other studies reviewed here, their records are truly impressive. Participants in SMPY are identified early in junior high school (or in mid-middle school by today's arrangements) on the basis of already-evident reasoning ability and motivation. They must also have strong verbal ability if they are to succeed at age 11 or 12 in college-level courses. SMPY has had a policy of finding out as much as possible about each participant, and then through counseling and tutoring, working to develop the youth's abilities. As Stanley (1977) pointed out years ago, acceleration was the mode chosen rather than enrichment, largely because none of the enrichment formats met the specialized academic needs of these gifted students, and it has apparently been the appropriate choice.

As with other longitudinal studies, those that followed the SMPY students were attentive to the social and emotional adjustment of these adolescents. Pollins (1983) and Richardson and Benbow (1990), mentioned earlier, found that the radical acceleration of these students did not generally have negative socioemotional effects in later years. However, Stanley (1991) pointed out that

> not working hard at social relationships over the early years sometimes results in a young man's or woman's becoming permanently immature socially; parental wisdom and continual help for the developing child seem crucial. Failing to develop nonacademic skills such as in athletics and the performing arts may limit the youth's personality development. (p. 69)

St. Louis's Star Students

In the post-Sputnik enthusiasm for high-powered education for everyone, but especially for the gifted, the St. Louis schools developed a special program for youngsters with IQ 140+ to begin in fifth grade and continue through the high school years (B. A. Kerr, 1985).

Ten years after high school graduation, there was a class reunion at which Kerr, by then a psychologist, was persuaded to undertake a follow-up study of this special group of gifted students.

As with Schwartz's study below, Kerr's principal effort was to find out the impact of the special program on the subjects' lives, especially the females. To her surprise, of the 24 female respondents reporting on their educational achievement, 25% had not earned an undergraduate college degree by age 29; half had earned their bachelor's degree but half of these were in education; four had master's degrees; and only two had professional degrees (one physician and one attorney) (p. 19). *All* of the 15 male respondents who supplied educational information had graduated from college, with one third of them earning professional degrees. Further, of the women, one third were homemakers and only four were in professional or semiprofessional occupations, in contrast to the males, all of whom were in professional or semiprofessional occupations (p. 20).

More disconcerting to Kerr seemed to be the young women's denial of giftedness, their lowering of aspirations to conform to sex role stereotypes, their acceptance of or adjustment to a reality in which they had not made great accomplishments, and yet their general insistence that they were happy in their lives. Kerr attributes this to the common finding in studies of the gifted that they are generally well-adjusted people, possibly better adjusted than the average. Further, according to Kerr,

> Being well-adjusted in a society in which women are expected to achieve less well than men, in which marriage and child raising are viewed as major accomplishments, demands calm adjustment, and the gifted woman complies. Also, because she is psychologically hardier than her "average" peers, the gifted woman may deal creatively with conflicts between her original goals and societal expectations and is, therefore, less likely to complain about her lifestyle than is the average woman. (pp. 26-27)

This acquiescence to reality seems a bit more forced in the mid-1970s than it would have in the mid-1950s or even early 1960s, when homemaking and child rearing were clearly the only appropriate roles for females. Guidance and career counseling were apparently inadequate even in as high-powered a program as the Accelerated Learning Program, and according to the responses to Kerr's questionnaire, "In most cases, no adult had affirmed the gifts of these women, raised their aspirations, or challenged them to attempt self-actualization" (pp. 32-33). The lowered self-concept of these young women because they felt they had not fulfilled their earlier promise thus stands in contrast to women who gained eminence as adults: They were regarded as "special" by adults significant in their young lives, and possibly of even greater importance, they refused to be limited by socially imposed barriers. It should be remembered, too, that most of the young women in this study were just approaching their 30th birthday and it would have been truly remarkable if they had made outstanding career achievements at that point in their lives.

Gifted Youths in Israel

Education of the gifted is especially important to developing nations, and Israel is one country that recognizes this need. R. M. Milgram (in press) reported on a group of such students over a tumultuous 18-year period that began shortly before the 1973 war with neighboring countries and that ended shortly before the 1991 Persian Gulf War.

The initial study was done when the subjects were members of the senior class at Tel Aviv High School. In the follow-up, current vocational and nonacademic talented accomplishments of the subjects as well as their leisure activities were compared with an Activities Inventory they had completed in the original study. Adult achievements were found to be more closely related to creative leisure activities and an unconventional predictors-creative thinking measure than to the more conventional predictors of achievement such as intelligence tests. In Milgram's view, this strongly argues for inclusion of measures of leisure activities in selection batteries.

Lighthouse in Racine

In 1975-1976, the Racine Unified School District, with the support of federal funds, identified the top-scoring 9% of its entering students in each major ethnic group as gifted, and randomly assigned the youngsters to an experimental (gifted treatment) or control (no special treatment) program. Of these, 91 were minority students, 24 of whom were in the gifted program and the balance in the control group. Twelve years later, 78 members of this original group were still in the Racine area. The results speak for themselves:

> Not one of the 24 minority students who were included in the gifted program dropped out. Of the 67 equally able

minority students who were not included in the Lighthouse Project, 30 (45%) dropped out. . . . The decision of which students to exclude was made randomly and therefore equitably—but the results were disastrously inequitable. (J. Smith, LeRose, & Clasen, 1991, p. 83)

Not only was there a difference in the percentage of dropouts, but of the 24 minority students in the Lighthouse Project in the class of 1988, 15 (or 63%) were in higher education, compared with 14 (21%) of the 67 who had been in the control group (J. Smith et al., 1991). Although this is a relatively small sample, the success of the project, and of a related program for academically talented students in Milwaukee, underscores the importance of providing appropriate educational opportunities to minority students from the time they enter school. As Smith and associates assert vigorously, "Anything else *'violates educational equity and is totally undefensible' "* (p. 83).

Gifted at Ogontz

Curiosity among faculty members at Penn State's Ogontz Campus who had participated in Projects GO (Gifted at Ogontz) and PATS (Potentially Academically Talented Students) with middle school students in the early 1980s (Schwartz & Fischman, 1984) led to the initiation of a follow-up study in summer 1992. GO included only identified gifted students, whereas PATS also included economically disadvantaged students who had been nominated as "potentially academically talented students."

Of the approximately 115 students who had attended these programs on campus either before or after their own school day or during the summer, current addresses could be located for only half the group. A short questionnaire was sent to these potential subjects in 1992, followed by an additional mailing and an advertisement in local newspapers, still yielding only 25 responses.

Fifteen of the respondents were male and 10 female, with a present age range of 21-25 years. None were married or had children. All had graduated from high school; 21 had already graduated from college, with 4 still attending; and 15 indicated that they were attending or planned to attend graduate school, with 2 more still deciding about that path. Fifteen subjects were employed full-time, three part-time, with some of these also among the continuing students. College majors were varied (as seen in Table 8.1), with several respondents indicating that a course in the gifted program had influenced their choice of major.

Table 8.1 College Majors ($N = 25$)

Engineering (any sub-type)	8
Science	4
Psychology	3
Social Sciences	3
Business fields	2
Communications	2
Education	1
Other	2

Of particular interest to the faculty members was the question of whether or not their efforts had had any real impact on these students. Accordingly, respondents were asked, "As you look back more than 10 years to your experience at Penn State Ogontz, how would you rate the value (on a scale of 1-10, with 10 highest) of that experience in influencing (a) your academic career? (b) your life to this point? (c) your self-esteem?" Answers ranged from 1-10 for academic career and self-esteem, and from 1-9 for their life to date (Table 8.2). (One respondent failed to respond to this question.)

Respondents were also asked whether they would recommend a similar program to middle school gifted students today, to which all but one answered yes. (The one negative response focused on the academic nature of the program.) The primary reason they gave was the opportunity for challenge. Specific comments included:

> "Absolutely *wonderful* experience. I remained excited about college throughout high school."

> "It was a chance to get exposure to both the university environment and many varied fields of study. It was a factor in my choice of major and eventually my career."

> "PATS was very mind-opening and instilled confidence and self-esteem and offered exposure to subjects in a very rewarding way."

> "Gifted students are frequently scorned or looked down upon because teachers don't know how to handle them. I think this is an excellent opportunity to let the students get positive reinforcement."

Table 8.2 Average and High Values for Areas of Influence (N = 24)

	Mean	Number High Values (8-10)
Academic career	5.42	7
Life to now	5.50	5
Self-esteem	6.96	12

"I remember being told it was very hard to get into a class even if you were already in the 'gifted' program and being *very* excited when I did.... It was also good to interact early with kids from other schools that we would later see in high school."

As encouraging as these long-term memories were, it was felt important also to ask for suggestions for gifted programs for the middle school age group. Here, too, the responses were enlightening:

"I felt that small class size was very important to my learning. It would be great to keep the number in each class to 5 or 6."

"I feel that they need these programs to keep them motivated and challenged, and to remind them that they have special talents that they should be proud of. I also think that having younger children working with similarly talented older children makes them feel more comfortable with their above average intelligence and maturity."

"Exceptional students don't need having their intellectual appetites whetted so much as they demand that the material they learn be useful."

Because participants in the two projects came from area parochial schools as well as public schools, one other comment should be noted:

"As a student in a relatively homogeneous parochial elementary school, I recall thinking that one of the most valuable aspects of the program was the opportunity to interact with students of more diverse backgrounds."

It is interesting to read these comments in light of those made by parents immediately following participation of their children and one year after participation. Some of the reasons given in the initial follow-up (a decade earlier) "were the positive response to the college environment, the opportunity to meet children from other schools and communities, and the feelings of adventure and being 'special' provided by the experience" (Schwartz & Fischman, 1984, p. 132). A year later, a highly significant parental response, especially in light of the lack of college experience of many of the parents, was that "aspirations had been raised to include a college education" (p. 132).

The respondents who noted that their home school teachers, and sometimes peers, did not know how to relate to them offered an important clue to the needs of potential and identified gifted students, as did those who called for more choice in minicourses. The recurrent themes of challenge and benefits to self-esteem found in these responses, as well as the evident achievement of the sample to date, support the value of special programming for gifted and talented students. Finally, it was noted by Schwartz and Fischman that for the staff of these projects, "an underlying objective was to stimulate joy in learning among youngsters at a critical point in their educational lives in an environment unfamiliar to them. This happened" (1984, p. 134). Ten years after the effort, for at least 25 of the participants, it did indeed "happen."

Conclusion

What do these longitudinal studies teach us about gifted children? Further, in what ways can what we have learned guide our educational efforts in the future? First things first. These studies indicate several things:

1. The gifted appear to have better-than-average physical and mental health and above-average longevity. (Whether this is at least partly attributable to their being smart enough to take care of their health is presently an unknown factor, but seems possible.)
2. The gifted had many interests as children and often continued some of their hobbies into adulthood as part of their career or as an avocation.
3. The gifted tend to have a constellation of characteristics that contribute to their achievement: initiative, self-motivation (the

ability to set goals), perseverance (task commitment), independence (internal locus of control), and self-confidence.
4. Most of the gifted had parental support for their efforts.
5. Acceleration had positive effects on the gifted in their personal, educational, and occupational lives.
6. Most of the gifted, and certainly the males among them, had higher than average occupational status as adults. This seems to be true to a lesser magnitude among the females, partly because of inadequate counseling and guidance, too few female models or mentors, and gender barriers or stereotypes that have persisted to some degree even to the present day.
7. The gifted have tended to be contributors to the world around them (with a very small percentage becoming dependent on society as criminals, or as hospitalized mentally ill).

Perhaps the three key points here are the self-direction of the gifted, the need for better counseling of the female gifted, and the fact that the gifted are contributors, not parasites or detractors. These studies certainly indicate that the gifted not only have within themselves the ingredients and the potential for being healthy and positive members of society, but also that they need the support of family *and* school to bring that potential to reality. The findings of these studies should also alert society in general and policymakers and educators in particular to the need to supply such support lest the potential be turned to destructive purposes or wasted altogether.

It should be evident, both from the longitudinal studies just reviewed and from the research literature cited throughout this book, that giftedness may be found in many settings and disguises. It is also apparent, from the previous chapter as well as this one, that helping the gifted to move toward fulfilling their potential need not be expensive in dollars. What is needed is the will to search for potential abilities and the willingness to draw out the talents of our youth for their own self-actualization as well as for the benefit of society.

9 Conclusion

There is virtually unanimous agreement among thinking people, when asked, that each human is unique. Despite overlapping experiences, genetic bonds, and commonalities in patterns of development, it is generally recognized that individuals arrive at the same point (whether we are discussing chronological age, grade level, or situation) with somewhat different expectations and perceptions. This recognition is verbalized when educators say that they provide for individual differences in their schools.

> In fact, it is at the core of middle school philosophy that middle school exists to deal with a wide range of physical, social, emotional, and intellectual maturity, and that no one strategy, plan, or practice will be adequate to deal with this population which at any given moment ranges from socially adept to socially clumsy, physically mature to physically immature, emotionally steady to emotionally turbulent, and *intellectually astute to intellectually dormant*. (Tomlinson, 1992, p. 208)

In reality, the middle schools do not necessarily serve their students in line with this philosophy, but neither does any other level for the most part. The philosophy then, if not the practice, is attuned to the transitional waves that overflow the middle school population. Among the gifted group, who tend to be more sensitive to the world around them than less gifted peers, there is often particular concern with finding an appropriate niche. Their academic expertise tends not to be valued by their peers; they have less and less in common with classmates who are less intellectually able than they;

and at the same time, they have the same need as their age peers to develop a sense of identity and positive self-concept. Being mainstreamed to avoid elitism does not appear to meet their needs or to conform to the middle school philosophy as stated. The gifted learn rather quickly that

> the culture and the community will support the kinds of activities that they find necessary, valuable and/or enjoyable. If they feel that a program is sufficiently necessary . . . , all sorts of objections are put aside as being relatively inconsequential. If, on the other hand, the community is not fully interested or involved in supporting such a program, all kinds of objections can be raised as to why these things should not be done, or cannot be done. (Gallagher, 1975, p. 84)

Grouping the "intellectually astute" in subjects where they are unusually able allows them to use, develop, and stretch their abilities. Grouping the "intellectually dormant" in those same subjects permits them to learn, develop, and use new abilities. Would we expect the first squad of the football team to sit patiently while those unable or unwilling to learn basic plays are being coached? Then why should this be done in mathematics or science or foreign-language classes? Further, such grouping for the "intellectually astute" will encourage them to remain in school rather than to be numbered among the 10% to 15% of high school dropouts who are gifted but bored (DeLeon & VandenBos, 1985). As dropouts, they are lost as contributing and creative members of society and may even become psychologically damaged.

In enumerating the personal qualities of the gifted, whether those easily found through test scores and course grades or those named here as the underidentified gifted, it becomes apparent that these characteristics are the very traits everyone says are valued in our society. We admire those who persevere at a task, those who are willing to take a chance (i.e., take risks), those who can solve sticky problems, those who can create something new, and those whose talents beautify our lives through sound and visual images. Without people like the gifted, virtually every aspect of our lives would be sorely impoverished and daily life would certainly be more labor intensive.

At the same time, we feel somewhat threatened by those who are different from ourselves, for we don't quite know in what ways to relate to them. This is true for some parents of the gifted and for their teachers and counselors as well. And if adults are disturbed by those who are different, how much more true it is that children and adolescents feel inadequate to deal with peers who may appear to be like them in age, size, and dress, yet think and behave in ways that are strange to them. We can ill afford, however, to pass amendments such as those presented by Vonnegut in an effort to make everyone appear to be equal.

Taken from another perspective, providing appropriate education for gifted and talented students (i.e., removing them from mainstreaming and lockstep situations) would enable other students to experience the success of being the highest scorer on a test or the most creative and to assume leadership roles in the classroom. This is similar in effect to the sex-segregated education, noted earlier, that provided opportunities for girls to assume roles that were less often available to them in coeducational schools. Further, as these opportunities to shine occur more often for average students, more of them may make the effort to achieve at a higher level, and some of these youngsters may turn out to be hidden gifted underachievers.

Psychologists and others interested in the education of the gifted also recognize the importance to national economic competitiveness of educating the gifted appropriately (DeAngelis, 1992). They further assert that improving the quality of education for gifted children will ultimately improve the quality of education for all students. As Albert Shanker (1993), president of the American Federation of Teachers, wrote,

> Suppose education reform results in all students' doing better but higher-achieving students' making much more progress than those at the bottom. Even though the gap between top and bottom would increase, those at the bottom would be much more employable than they are now. In fact, they could qualify for jobs that are now moving to other countries because our young people don't have the skills to do them. Most people would find this a big step forward. (p. E7)

Moreover, as Tomlinson and Callahan (1992) suggested, education of the gifted can provide models for education in general such as individualization, multiple modes of instruction, and a variety of teaching models, and can also set a standard for excellence rather than mediocrity.

A Delphi study of 29 experts in the education of the gifted drew attention to six issues as top priorities in this field: (a) curriculum for the gifted, (b) procedures for identifying gifted children, (c) selection and training of teachers of the gifted, (d) working with special populations of gifted, (e) ascertaining goals of programs for the gifted, and (f) defining the term "gifted" (Cramer, 1991). Their concerns further specify that at the local level, there is a responsibility to "ensure that a differentiated curriculum be provided to gifted students" and that in-service training on the characteristics and needs of all gifted students "should be provided to teachers of *all* children" (p. 90). As Cramer and others cited here have testified, the gifted are the losers if mainstreamed without concern for their needs, whereas all students are the beneficiaries if improved educational techniques designed for the gifted are then incorporated into mainstream classrooms.

The need to sensitize all teachers to the characteristics and needs of gifted and talented students should be extended as well to school counselors. Together, these two groups should be key sources of support and information for gifted children and for their parents. They should also be advocates in the community for these students, seeking mentors and resources to help them develop their potential. If educators do not foster giftedness, who will?

> In a world of fierce international competition, the extent to which a country's standard of living will grow (or whether it will grow at all) may depend on how much that country is willing to invest in educating its children and on the nature of the educational investments that it selects. Given the extreme importance of the cognitive environment provided during infancy and toddlerhood it is appropriate that we commit ourselves to providing children with as good an educational environment during the first and second years of their lives as we now provide to young men and women during their third and fourth years of college. (Storfer, 1990, p. 521)

It must be recognized that gifted and talented children are complex beings who must be handled as "whole children" rather than as the disembodied "gifted." As Zigler and Farber (1985) pointed out, "Schooling is much more than academic learning. It also involves the social and emotional training that ultimately shapes a person and the place he or she will assume in society" (p. 404). This philosophy places a great responsibility on educational decisionmakers and implementers.

Finally, providing appropriate special education for the gifted is actually a cost-saving practice, for the ultimate return is much greater than the cost. "A few instructional minutes spent with a brilliant youth can produce amazing results," wrote Stanley. "This contrasts sharply with the much greater amount of time that one must devote to a slow learner in order to get even moderate gains" (1977, p. 103). His view is somewhat biased, and perhaps not "politically correct" 16 years later, but it still contains some truth. This does not mean that education of slower students should be eliminated, but rather that some funds should be provided to others who can also profit from special assistance.

A classroom teacher in South Dakota has pointed out the irony of reducing or eliminating programs for gifted and talented students at the same time that the public is crying out about the lack of excellence in our schools and of competitiveness in the commercial and scientific worlds. She asks, "What better way to meet the challenges of the next century than by enabling our brightest students to go as far as possible in their learning? Why not give them the tools they need to exploit the technology of tomorrow?" (McIntyre, 1992, p. 39).

Why not, indeed?

References

Abbott, J. A. (1982). An anthropological approach to the identification of Navajo gifted children. In *Identifying and educating the disadvantaged gifted talented: Selected proceedings from the Fifth National Conference on Disadvantaged Gifted/Talented* (pp. 7-18). Ventura, CA: Ventura County Superintendent of Schools Office.

Abra, J., & Valentine-French, S. (1991). Gender differences in creative achievement: A survey of explanations. *Genetic, Social, and General Psychology Monographs, 117*, 235-284.

Abroms, K. I. (1985). Social giftedness and its relationship with intellectual giftedness. In J. Freeman (Ed.), *The psychology of gifted children* (pp. 201-218). New York: John Wiley.

Anastasi, A., & Foley, J. P., Jr. (1958). *Differential psychology.* New York: Macmillan.

Armour-Thomas, E. (1992). Intellectual assessment of children from culturally diverse populations. *School Psychology Review, 21*, 552-565.

The Association for the Gifted. (1989). *Standards for programs involving the gifted and talented.* Reston, VA: Council for Exceptional Children.

Astin, H. S., & Leland, C. (1991). *Women of influence, women of vision.* San Francisco: Jossey-Bass.

Ayles, R. (1992). Gifted girls: A case of wasted talent? In F. J. Monks, M. W. Katzko, & H. W. Van Boxtel (Eds.), *Education of the gifted in Europe: Theoretical and research issues* (pp. 157-161). Amsterdam: Swets & Zeitlinger.

Baldwin, A. Y. (1985). Programs for the gifted and talented: Issues concerning minority populations. In F. D. Horowitz & M. O'Brien (Eds.), *The gifted and talented: Developmental perspectives* (pp. 223-249). Washington, DC: American Psychological Association.

Barber, B. R. (1992). *An aristocracy of everyone: The politics of education and the future of America.* New York: Ballantine.

Baska, L. K. (1989). Characteristics and needs of the gifted. In J. Feldhusen, J. Van Tassel-Baska, & K. Seeley (Eds.), *Excellence in educating the gifted* (pp. 15-28). Denver: Love.

Bathgate, A. J., & Connelly, L. A. (1991). Challenging gifted students with Michener's *The Source* in a history class. *Journal of Reading, 35*(1), 48-49.

Bell, L. A. (1989). Something's wrong here and it's not me: Challenging the dilemmas that block girls' success. *Journal for the Education of the Gifted, 12,* 118-130.

Bentsen, C. (1979, June 18). The brightest kids. *New York,* pp. 36-40.

Bermúdez, A. B., & Rakow, S. J. (1990, Summer). Analyzing teachers' perceptions of identification procedures for gifted and talented Hispanic Limited English Proficiency (LEP) students at-risk. *Journal of Educational Issues of Language Minority Students, 7,* 21-33.

Birch, J. W. (1984). Is *any* identification procedure necessary? *Gifted Child Quarterly, 28,* 157-161.

Bireley, M. (1991). The paradoxical needs of the disabled gifted. In M. Bireley & J. Genshaft (Eds.), *Understanding the gifted adolescent: Educational, developmental, and multicultural issues* (pp. 163-175). New York: Teachers College Press.

Bogat, G. A., & Redner, R. L. (1985). How mentoring affects the professional development of women in psychology. *Professional Psychology, 16,* 851-859.

Boodoo, G. M., Bradley, C. L., Frontera, R. L., Pitts, J. R., & Wright, L. B. (1989). A survey of procedures used for identifying gifted learning disabled children. *Gifted Child Quarterly, 33,* 110-114.

Booth, L. (1980). Motivating gifted students through a shared-governance apprentice/mentor program. *Roeper Review, 3*(1), 11-13.

Braddock, J. H., & McPartland, J. M. (1993). Education of early adolescents. In L. Darling-Hammond (Ed.), *Review of Research in Education, 19,* 135-170. Washington, DC: American Education Research Association.

Brody, L. E., Assouline, S. G., & Stanley, J. C. (1990). Five years of early entrants: Predicting successful achievement in college. *Gifted Child Quarterly, 34,* 138-142.

Brooks, R. (1980). Gifted delinquents. *Educational Research, 22,* 212-220.

Brown, W. K., & Rhodes, W. A. (1991). Factors that promote invulnerability and resiliency in at-risk children. In W. A. Rhodes & W. K. Brown (Eds.), *Why some children succeed despite the odds* (pp. 171-177). New York: Praeger.

Bull, B. L. (1985). Eminence and precocity: An examination of the justification of education for the gifted and talented. *Teachers College Record, 87*(1), 1-19.

Callahan, C. M. (1980). The gifted girl: An anomaly? *Roeper Review, 2*(3), 16-20.

Callahan, C. M., Cornell, D. G., & Loyd, B. (1990). Perceived competence and parent-adolescent communication in high ability adolescent females. *Journal for the Education of the Gifted, 13*, 256-269.

Chetelat, F. J. (1981). Visual arts education for the gifted elementary level art student. *Gifted Child Quarterly, 25*, 154-158.

Chicago student wins top science prize. (1993, March 9). *The New York Times*, p. A17.

Christopherson, S. L. (1979). *Developmental placement of intellectually gifted children*. Paper presented at the Annual Meeting of the American Psychological Association.

Clark, G. A., & Zimmerman, E. D. (1988). Views of self, family background, and school: Interviews with artistically talented students. *Gifted Child Quarterly, 32*, 340-346.

Clinkenbeard, P. R. (1989). The motivation to win: Negative aspects of success at competition. *Journal for the Education of the Gifted, 12*, 293-305.

Clinkenbeard, P. R. (1991). Unfair expectations: A pilot study of middle school students' comparisons of gifted and regular classes. *Journal for the Education of the Gifted, 15*, 56-63.

Colon, P. J., & Treffinger, D. J. (1980). Providing for the gifted in the regular classroom—Am I really MAD? *Roeper Review, 3*(2), 18-21.

Congressional Record. (1978, October 10). H-12179.

Cornell, D. G. (1990). High ability students who are unpopular with their peers. *Gifted Child Quarterly, 34*, 155-158.

Cox, A. (1980, February). Teaching gifted students in regular classrooms. *Education Digest*, pp. 17-19.

Cramer, R. H. (1991). The education of gifted children in the United States: A Delphi study. *Gifted Child Quarterly, 35*, 84-91.

Cramond, B., & Martin, C. E. (1987). Inservice and preservice teachers' attitudes toward the academically brilliant. *Gifted Child Quarterly, 31*, 15-19.

Cramond, B., Martin, C. E., & Shaw, E. L. (1990). Generalizibility of creative problem solving procedures to real-life problems. *Journal for the Education of the Gifted, 13*, 141-155.

Cropley, A., & McLeod, J. (1986). Preparing teachers of the gifted. *International Review of Education, 32*, 125-136.

Csikszentmihalyi, M. (1993). Contexts of optimal growth in childhood. *Daedalus, 122*(1), 31-56.

Cummings, M. A., & Merrell, K. W. (1993). K-ABC score patterns of Sioux children: Mental processing styles, effects of school attendance, and relationship between raw scores and age. *Journal of Psychoeducational Assessment, 11*, 38-45.

Davidson, K. L. (1992). A comparison of Native American and white students' cognitive strengths as measured by the Kaufman Assessment Battery for Children. *Roeper Review, 14*, 111-115.

DeAngelis, T. (1992, April). Conference explores issues of giftedness. *APA Monitor*, pp. 42-43.

DeLeon, P. H., & VandenBos, G. R. (1985). Public policy and advocacy on behalf of the gifted and talented. In F. D. Horowitz & M. O'Brien (Eds.), *The gifted and talented: Developmental perspectives* (pp. 409-435). Washington, DC: American Psychological Association.

Delisle, J. R. (1990). The gifted adolescent at risk: Strategies and resources for suicide prevention among gifted youth. *Journal for the Education of the Gifted, 13*, 212-228.

Demetrulias, D. M. (1992). Developing intellectual creativity through children's literature for preschoolers through third grade. *Education, 112*, 464-469.

Dillon, S. (1993, April 5). New York City readies 37 specialized schools. *The New York Times*, pp. A1, B6.

Editors. (1990). Letters. *Science News, 138*, 339.

Edlind, E. P., & Haensley, P. A. (1985). Gifts of mentorships. *Gifted Child Quarterly, 29*, 55-60.

Encyclopedia of American Ethnic Groups. (1975). Cambridge, MA: Harvard University Press.

Erikson, E. H. (1960). *Childhood and Society.* New York: Norton.

Farley, F. (1991). The type-T personality. In L. Kipsett & L. L. Mitnick (Eds.), *Self-regulatory behavior and risk taking: Causes and consequences* (pp. 371-382). Norwood, NJ: Ablex.

Farmer, H. S. (1987). A multivariate model for explaining gender differences in career and achievement motivation. *Educational Researcher, 16*(2), 5-9.

Feagin, J. R. (1989). *Racial and ethnic relations* (3rd ed.). Englewood Cliffs, NJ: Prentice-Hall.

Feldhusen, J. F. (1983). Eclecticism: A comprehensive approach to education of the gifted. In C. P. Benbow & J. C. Stanley (Eds.), *Academic precocity: Aspects of its development* (pp. 192-204). Baltimore, MD: Johns Hopkins University Press.

Feldhusen, J. F. (1991). Effects of programs for the gifted: A search for evidence. In W. T. Southern & E. D. Jones (Eds.), *The academic acceleration of gifted children* (pp. 133-147). New York: Teachers College Press.

Feldhusen, J. F., Asher, J. W., & Hoover, S. M. (1984). Problems in the identification of giftedness, talent, or ability. *Gifted Child Quarterly, 28,* 149-151.

Feldhusen, J. F., & Huffman, L. E. (1988). Practicum experiences in an educational program for teachers of the gifted. *Journal for the Education of the Gifted, 12*(1), 34-45.

Feldman, D. (1986). *Nature's gambit.* New York: Basic Books.

Feldman, R. D. (1982). *Whatever happened to the Quiz Kids?* Chicago: Chicago Review Press.

Festinger, L. A. (1954). A theory of social comparison processes. *Human Relations, 7,* 117-140.

Feuerstein, R. (1980). *Instrumental enrichment: An intervention program for cognitive modifiability.* Baltimore, MD: University Park Press.

Fishkin, A. (1993, February). Education reform, gifted students, and creativity. *Celebrate Creativity, 4*(1), 6-7.

Fletcher, G. H., & Wooddell, G. D. (1980). Milford Futurology Program: Effective education for gifted ninth grade students. *Roeper Review, 3*(1), 15-18.

Flynn, J. R. (1991). *Asian Americans: Achievement beyond IQ.* Hillsdale, NJ: Lawrence Erlbaum.

Ford, D. Y. (1993). Support for the achievement ideology and determinants of underachievement as perceived by gifted, above-average, and average Black students. *Journal for the Education of the Gifted, 16,* 280-298.

Ford, D. Y., Harris, J., III, & Schuerger, J. M. (1993). Racial identity development among gifted Black students: Counseling issues and concerns. *Journal of Counseling and Development, 71,* 409-417.

Frasier, M. M. (1991). Disadvantaged and culturally diverse students. *Journal for the Education of the Gifted, 14,* 234-245.

Frydman, M., & Lynn, R. (1992). The general intelligence and spatial abilities of gifted young Belgian chess players. *British Journal of Psychology, 83,* 233-235.

Gallagher, J. J. (1975). *Teaching the gifted child* (2nd ed.). Boston: Allyn & Bacon.

Gallagher, J. J. (1986). A proposed federal role: Education of gifted children. *Gifted Child Quarterly, 30,* 43-46.

Gallagher, J. J. (1988). National agenda for educating gifted students: Statement of priorities. *Exceptional Children, 55,* 107-114.

Gallagher, J. J. (1990). Editorial: The public and professional perception of the emotional status of gifted children. *Journal for the Education of the Gifted, 13,* 202-211.

Gallagher, J. J. (1991). Personal patterns of underachievement. *Journal for the Education of the Gifted, 14,* 221-233.

Gallucci, N. T. (1989). Personality assessment with children of superior intelligence: Divergence versus psychopathology. *Journal of Personality Assessment, 53,* 749-760.

Garcia, R. L. (1991). *Teaching in a pluralistic society: Concepts, models, strategies* (2nd ed.). New York: HarperCollins.

Gardner, H. (1983). *Frames of mind: The theory of multiple intelligences.* New York: Basic Books.

Griffin, J. B. (1992). Catching the dream for gifted children of color. *Gifted Child Quarterly, 36,* 126-130.

Griggs, S. A. (1991). Counseling gifted children with different learning-style preferences. In R. M. Milgram (Ed.), *Counseling gifted and talented children: A guide for teachers, counselors, and parents* (pp. 53-74). Norwood, NJ: Ablex.

Gross, M. U. M. (1989). The pursuit of excellence or the search for intimacy? The forced-choice dilemma of gifted youth. *Roeper Review, 11,* 189-194.

Gross, M. U. M. (1992). The use of radical acceleration in cases of extreme intellectual precocity. *Gifted Child Quarterly, 36,* 91-99.

Grossberg, I. N., & Cornell, D. G. (1988). Relationship between personality adjustment and high intelligence: Terman versus Hollingworth. *Exceptional Children, 55,* 266-272.

Halpern, D. F. (1992). *Sex differences in cognitive abilities* (2nd ed.). Hillsdale, NJ: Lawrence Erlbaum.

Halsted, J. W. (1988). *Guiding gifted readers from preschool through high school: A handbook for parents, teachers, counselors, and librarians.* Columbus, OH: Ohio Psychology Publishing.

Handel, R. D. (1982). Teachers of gifted girls: Are there differences in classroom management? *Journal for the Education of the Gifted, 6*(2), 86-97.

Harvey, S., & Seeley, K. R. (1984). An investigation of the relationships among intellectual and creative abilities, extracurricular activities, achievement, and giftedness in a delinquent population. *Gifted Child Quarterly, 28,* 73-79.

Hayes, M. L., & Sloat, R. S. (1990). Suicide and the gifted adolescent. *Journal for the Education of the Gifted, 13,* 229-244.

Heid, M. K. (1983). Characteristics and special needs of the gifted student in mathematics. *The Mathematics Teacher, 76,* 221-226.

Higham, S. J., & Navarre, J. (1984). Gifted adolescent females require differential treatment. *Journal for the Education of the Gifted, 8*(1), 43-58.

Hildreth, G. H. (1952). *Educating gifted children at Hunter College Elementary School.* New York: Harper.

Hoge, R. D., & McSheffrey, R. (1991). An investigation of self-concept in gifted children. *Exceptional Children, 57,* 238-245.

Hollingworth, L. S. (1940). *Public addresses.* Lancaster, PA: Science Press.
Hollingworth, L. S. (1942). *Children above 180 IQ.* New York: World Book.
Hong, E., Whiston, S. C., & Milgram, R. M. (1993). Leisure activities in career guidance for gifted and talented adolescents: A validation study of the Tel-Aviv Activities Inventory. *Gifted Child Quarterly, 37,* 65-68.
Horner, M. (1970). Femininity and successful achievement: A basic inconsistency. In J. Bardwick, E. Douvan, M. Horner, & D. Guttman (Eds.), *Feminine personality and conflict* (pp. 45-74). Brookline, CA: Brooks/Cole.
Howard, S. W., Ault, M. M., Knowlton, H. E., & Swall, R. A. (1992). Distance education: Promises and cautions for special education. *Teacher Education and Special Education, 15,* 275-283.
In a minority district in Maryland, a magnet school that really draws. (1993, March 3). *The New York Times,* p. B13.
Isser, N., & Schwartz, L. L. (1985). *The American school and the melting pot: Minority self-esteem and public education.* Bristol, IN: Wyndham Hall.
Janos, P. M., Sanfilippo, S. M., & Robinson, N. M. (1986). "Underachievement" among markedly accelerated college students. *Journal of Youth and Adolescence, 15,* 303-313.
Jones, E. D., & Southern, W. T. (1991). Conclusions about acceleration: Echoes of debate. In W. T. Southern & E. D. Jones (Eds.), *The academic acceleration of gifted children* (pp. 223-228). New York: Teachers College Press.
Jordan, M. (1993, Nov. 5). U.S. chastises "ambivalence, neglect" of gifted students. *The Philadelphia Inquirer,* p. A15.
Kaplan, C. (1992). Ceiling effects in assessing high-IQ children with the WPPSI-R. *Journal of Clinical Child Psychology, 21,* 403-406.
Karnes, F. A., & Marquardt, R. G. (1988). The Pennsylvania Supreme Court decision on gifted education. *Gifted Child Quarterly, 32,* 360-361.
Karnes, F. A., & Meriweather-Bean, S. (1991). Leadership and gifted adolescents. In M. Bireley, & J. Genshaft (Eds.), *Understanding the gifted adolescent: Educational, developmental, and multicultural issues* (pp. 122-138). New York: Teachers College Press.
Karnes, F. A., & Whorton, J. E. (1991). Teacher certification and endorsement in gifted education: Past, present, and future. *Gifted Child Quarterly, 35,* 148-150.
Kaslow, F. W., & Schwartz, L. L. (1987). *The dynamics of divorce: A life cycle perspective.* New York: Brunner/Mazel.
Kaufmann, F. A. (1981). The 1964-68 Presidential Scholars: A follow-up study. *Exceptional Children, 48,* 164-169.

Kaufmann, F. A., Harrel, G., Milam, C. P., Woolverton, N., & Miller, J. (1986). The nature, role, and influence of mentors in the lives of gifted adults. *Journal of Counseling and Development, 64*, 576-578.

Keirouz, K. S. (1990). Concerns of parents of gifted children: A research review. *Gifted Child Quarterly, 34*, 56-63.

Kerr, B. A. (1985). *Smart girls, gifted women.* Columbus, OH: Ohio Psychology.

Kerr, B., Colangelo, N., Maxey, J., & Christensen, P. (1992). Characteristics of academically talented minority students. *Journal of Counseling and Development, 70*, 606-609.

Kierstead, F. D., & Wagner, P. A., Jr. (1993). *The ethical, legal, and multicultural foundations of teaching.* Madison, WI: WCB Brown & Benchmark.

Kitano, M. K. (1991). A multicultural educational perspective on serving the culturally diverse gifted. *Journal for the Education of the Gifted, 15*, 4-19.

Kolloff, P. B., & Feldhusen, J. F. (1984). The effects of enrichment on self-concept and creative thinking. *Gifted Child Quarterly, 28*, 53-57.

Kolloff, P. B., & Moore, A. D. (1989). Effects of summer programs on the self-concepts of gifted children. *Journal for the Education of the Gifted, 12*, 268-276.

Kornhaber, M., Krechevsky, M., & Gardner, H. (1990). Engaging intelligence. *Educational Psychologist, 25*, 177-199.

Kwan, P. C. F. (1993). Singaporean gifted adolescents under scrutiny: The gender factor. *International Review of Education, 39*(3), 161-182.

Laffoon, K. S., Jenkins-Friedman, R., & Tollefson, N. (1989). Causal attributions of underachieving gifted, achieving gifted, and nongifted students. *Journal for the Education of the Gifted, 13*, 4-21.

Lamb, J., & Daniels, R. (1993). Gifted girls in a rural community: Math attitudes and career options. *Exceptional Children, 59*, 513-517.

Lathlaen, P. (1990). The National Board for Professional Teaching Standards and possible implications for gifted education. *Journal for the Education of the Gifted, 14*, 50-65.

Lembke, R. C. (1992). Deadly praise. *Pi Lambda Theta Newsletter, 37*(3), 2, 4.

Levy, P. S. (1981). The story of Marie, David, Richard, Jane, and John: Teaching gifted children in the regular classroom. *Teaching Exceptional Children, 13*, 136-142.

Lewin, K. (1951). *Field theory in social science.* New York: Harper.

Lewin, K. (1954). Behavior and development as a function of the total situation. In L. Carmichael (Ed.), *Manual of Child Psychology* (2nd ed., pp. 918-970). New York: John Wiley.

Lewis, L. H. (1985). Old patterns: Changing the paradigm. *Educational Horizons, 63*(3), 129-132.

Lupkowski, A. E., Whitmore, M., & Ramsay, A. (1992). The impact of early entrance to college on self-esteem: A preliminary study. *Gifted Child Quarterly, 36,* 87-90.

Lynch, S. J., & Mills, C. J. (1990). The Skills Reinforcement Project (SRP): An academic program for high potential minority youth. *Journal for the Education of the Gifted, 13,* 364-379.

Lynch, S. J., & Mills, C. J. (1993). Identifying and preparing disadvantaged and minority youth for high-level academic achievement. *Contemporary Educational Psychology, 18,* 66-76.

Manegold, C. S. (1993, April 8). To Crystal, 12, school serves no purpose. *The New York Times,* pp. A1, B7.

Márquez, J. A., Bermúdez, A. B., & Rakow, S. J. (1992, Spring). Incorporating community perceptions in the identification of gifted and talented Hispanic students. *Journal of Educational Issues of Language Minority Students, 10,* 117-130.

Marsh, H. W. (1991). Failure of high-ability high schools to deliver academic benefits commensurate with their students' ability levels. *American Educational Research Journal, 28,* 445-480.

Matarazzo, J. D., & Pankratz, L. D. (1980). Intelligence. In R. H. Woody (Ed.), *Encyclopedia of clinical assessment* (Vol. 2, pp. 697-713). San Francisco: Jossey-Bass.

Matthews, M. (1992, October). Gifted students talk about cooperative learning. *Educational Leadership, 50,* 48-50.

McCarney, S. B. (1987). *Gifted evaluation scale.* Columbia, MO: Hawthorne Educational Services.

McIntyre, M. (1992, October). Should schools eliminate gifted and talented programs?: NO. *NEA Today,* p. 39.

McShane, D. A., & Berry, J. W. (1988). Native North Americans: Indian and Inuit abilities. In S. H. Irvine & J. W. Berry (Eds.), *Human abilities in cultural context* (pp. 385-426). Cambridge, UK: Cambridge University Press.

McShane, D. A., & Plas, J. M. (1984). The cognitive functioning of American Indian children: Moving from the WISC to the WISC-R. *School Psychology Review, 13,* 61-73.

Mead, M. (1935). Sex and achievement. *Forum, 94,* 302.

Mercer, J. R., & Lewis, J. F. (1979). *System of multicultural pluralistic assessment: Technical manual.* New York: Psychological Corporation.

Middlebrooks, M. W., & Strong, J. H. (1982). Project Career. *Roeper Review, 5*(2) 36-38.

Milgram, N. C. (1989). The SEEK (Summit Educational Enrichment for Kids) pull-out program: A boon and not a bane to teaching gifted children in regular classrooms. In R. M. Milgram (Ed.),

Teaching gifted and talented learners in regular classrooms (pp. 147-166). Springfield, IL: Charles C. Thomas.

Milgram, R. M. (Ed.) (1989a). *Teaching gifted and talented learners in regular classrooms.* Springfield, IL: Charles C. Thomas.

Milgram, R. M. (1989b). Teaching gifted and talented children in regular classrooms: An impossible dream or a full-time solution for a full-time problem? In R. M. Milgram (Ed.), *Teaching gifted and talented learners in regular classrooms* (pp. 7-32). Springfield, IL: Charles C. Thomas.

Milgram, R. M. (Ed.). (1991a). *Counseling gifted and talented children: A guide for teachers, counselors, and parents.* Norwood, NJ: Ablex.

Milgram, R. M. (1991b). Counseling gifted and talented children and youth: Who, where, what, and how? In R. M. Milgram (Ed.), *Counseling gifted and talented children: A guide for teachers, counselors, and parents* (pp. 7-21). Norwood, NJ: Ablex.

Milgram, R. M. (1992). Identifying gifted and talented children and adolescents around the world. In U. P. Gielen, L. L. Adler, & N. A. Milgram (Eds.), *Psychology in international perspective* (pp. 233-248). Amsterdam: Swets & Zeitlinger.

Milgram, R. M. (in press). Predicting outcomes of giftedness through intrinsically motivated behavior in adolescence. In S. G. Isaksen, M. C. Murdock, R. L. Firestien, & D. J. Treffinger (Eds.). *Nurturing and developing creativity: The emergence of a discipline.* Norwood, NJ: Ablex.

Milgram, R. M., & Goldring, E. B. (1991). Special education options for gifted and talented learners. In R. M. Milgram (Ed.), *Counseling gifted and talented children: A guide for teachers, counselors, and parents* (pp. 23-36). Norwood, NJ: Ablex.

Minner, S. (1990). Teacher evaluations of case descriptions of LD gifted children. *Gifted Child Quarterly, 34,* 37-39.

Mitchell, B. M., & Williams, W. G. (1987). Education of the gifted and talented in the world community. *Phi Delta Kappan, 68*(7), 531-534.

Monks, F. J. (1991). General introduction: From conception to realization. In F. J. Monks, M. W. Katzko, & H. W. van Boxtel (Eds.), *Education of the gifted in Europe: Theoretical and research issues* (pp. 13-21). Amsterdam: Swets & Zeitlinger.

Mulhern, J. D. (1978). The gifted child in the regular classroom. *Roeper Review, 1*(1), 3-6.

Naglieri, J. A. (1984). Concurrent and predictive validity of the Kaufman Assessment Battery for Children with a Navajo sample. *Journal of School Psychology, 22,* 373-380.

Navarre, J. (1980). Is what is good for the gander, good for the goose: Should gifted girls receive differential treatment? *Roeper Review, 2*(3), 21-25.

Nelson, J. G. (1992). Class clowns as a function of the Type T psychobiological personality. *Personality and Individual Differences, 13,* 1247-1248.

Nelson, K. C., & Prindle, N. (1992). Gifted teacher competencies: Ratings by rural principals and teachers compared. *Journal for the Education of the Gifted, 15,* 357-369.

Noble, K. D., & Drummond, J. E. (1992). But what about the prom? Students' perceptions of early college entrance. *Gifted Child Quarterly, 36,* 106-111.

Ortiz, V. Z., & Gonzalez, A. (1989). Validation of a short form of the WISC-R with accelerated and gifted Hispanic students. *Gifted Child Quarterly, 33,* 152-155.

Osborne, J. K., & Byrnes, D. A. (1990). Identifying gifted and talented students in an alternative learning center. *Gifted Child Quarterly, 34,* 143-146.

Patton, J. M. (1992). Assessment and identification of African-American learners with gifts and talents. *Exceptional Children, 59,* 150-159.

Perez, G. S. (1980). Perceptions of the young gifted child. *Roeper Review, 3*(2), 9-11.

Perrone, P. (1986). Guidance needs of gifted children, adolescents, and adults. *Journal of Counseling and Development, 64,* 564-566.

Pollins, L. D. (1983). The effects of acceleration on the social and emotional development of gifted students. In C. P. Benbow & J. C. Stanley (Eds.), *Academic precocity: Aspects of its development* (pp. 160-178). Baltimore, MD: Johns Hopkins University Press.

Radford, J. (1990). *Child prodigies and exceptional early achievers.* New York: Free Press.

Redding, R. E. (1990). Learning preferences and skill patterns among under-achieving gifted adolescents. *Gifted Child Quarterly, 34,* 72-75.

Reis, S. M., & Renzulli, J. S. (1992, October). Using curriculum compacting to challenge the above-average. *Educational Leadership, 50,* 51-57.

Renzulli, J. S. (1975). Talent potential in minority group students. In W. S. Barbe & J. S. Renzulli (Eds.), *Psychology and education of the gifted* (pp. 411-423). New York: Irvington.

Renzulli, J. S. (1977). *The Enrichment Triad Model: A guide for developing defensible programs for the gifted and talented.* Mansfield Center, CT: Creative Learning Press.

Renzulli, J. S. (1984). The Triad/Revolving Door System: A research-based approach to identification and programming for the gifted and talented. *Gifted Child Quarterly, 28,* 163-171.

Renzulli, J. S., & Reis, S. (1991, November 21). Workshop on the gifted and talented, Allentown, PA.

Richardson, T. M., & Benbow, C. P. (1990). Long-term effects of acceleration on the social-emotional adjustment of mathematically precocious youth. *Journal of Educational Psychology, 82,* 464-470.

Rimm, S. B., & Lovance, K. J. (1992). The use of subject and grade skipping for the prevention and reversal of underachievement. *Gifted Child Quarterly, 36,* 100-105.

Rimm, S. B., & Lowe, B. (1988). Family environments of underachieving gifted students. *Gifted Child Quarterly, 32,* 353-359.

Robinson, N. M., & Janos, P. M. (1986). Psychological adjustment in a college-level program of marked academic acceleration. *Journal of Youth and Adolescence, 15*(1), 51-60.

Rogers, J. A., & Nielson, A. B. (1993). Gifted children and divorce: A study of the literature on the incidence of divorce in families with gifted children. *Journal for the Education of the Gifted, 16,* 251-267.

Rogers, K. B., & Kimpston, R. D. (1992, October). Acceleration: What we do vs. what we know. *Educational Leadership, 50,* 58-61.

Ross, A., & Parker, M. (1980). Academic and social self concepts of the academically gifted. *Exceptional Children, 47*(2), 6-10.

Runco, M. A. (1986). Maximal performance on divergent thinking tests by gifted, talented, and nongifted children. *Psychology in the Schools, 23,* 308-315.

Runco, M. A. (1992). Review: Children's divergent thinking and creative ideation. *Developmental Review, 12,* 233-264.

Runco, M. A., & Albert, R. S. (1986). Exceptional giftedness in early adolescence and intrafamilial divergent thinking. *Journal of Youth and Adolescence, 15,* 335-344.

Salerno-Sonnenberg, N. (1993, January 17). Sunday morning. CBS-TV.

Sato, I. S. (1988). The C^3 Model: Resolving critical curricular issues through Comprehensive Curriculum Coordination. *Journal for the Education of the Gifted, 11*(2), 92-115.

Sawyer, R. N., DeLong, M. R., & von Brock, A. B. (1987). By-mail learning options for academically talented middle-school youth. *Gifted Child Quarterly, 31,* 118-120.

Schack, G. D., & Starko, A. J. (1990). Identification of gifted students: An analysis of criteria preferred by preservice teachers, classroom teachers, and teachers of the gifted. *Journal for the Education of the Gifted, 13,* 346-363.

Schneider, S. (1991, February). Underachievement: Developing student potential. *PAGE Bulletin,* p. 1.

Schwartz, L. L. (1972). *Educational psychology: Focus on the learner.* Boston: Holbrook.

Schwartz, L. L. (1980). Advocacy for the neglected gifted: Females. *Gifted Child Quarterly, 24*, 113-117.
Schwartz, L. L. (1984). *Exceptional students in the mainstream.* Belmont, CA: Wadsworth.
Schwartz, L. L. (1987, April). *Gifted daughters.* Paper presented at the annual meeting of the Pennsylvania Association for Gifted Children, Philadelphia.
Schwartz, L. L. (1991). Guiding gifted girls. In R. M. Milgram (Ed.), *Counseling gifted and talented children: A guide for teachers, counselors, and parents* (pp. 143-160). Norwood, NJ: Ablex.
Schwartz, L. L., & Fischman, R. (1984). Integrating the potentially able and the exceptionally able. *Gifted Child Quarterly, 28*, 130-134.
Scott, M. (1988). Gifted-talented-creative (G/T/C) children's development: Four parenting keys to help develop potential. *Creative Child and Adult Quarterly, 13*(1), 7-9, 16.
Scott, M. S., Perou, R., Urbano, R., Hogan, A., & Gold, S. (1992). The identification of giftedness: A comparison of white, Hispanic, and black families. *Gifted Child Quarterly, 36*, 131-139.
Sears, P. S., & Barbee, A. H. (1977). Career and life satisfactions among Terman's gifted women. In J. C. Stanley, W. C. George, & C. H. Solano (Eds.), *The gifted and the creative: A fifty-year perspective* (pp. 28-65). Baltimore, MD: Johns Hopkins University Press.
Seeley, K. (1989a). Facilitators for the gifted. In J. Feldhusen, J. Van Tassel-Baska, & K. Seeley (Eds.), *Excellence in educating the gifted* (pp. 279-298). Denver: Love.
Seeley, K. (1989b). Underachieving and handicapped gifted. In J. Feldhusen, J. Van Tassel-Baska, & K. Seeley (Eds.), *Excellence in educating the gifted* (pp. 29-37). Denver: Love.
Shanker, A. (1993, June 11). Where we stand: Two kinds of equity. *The New York Times*, p. E7.
Shmurak, C. B., & Handler, B. S. (1992). "Castle of science": Mount Holyoke College and the preparation of women in chemistry, 1837-1941. *History of Education Quarterly, 32*, 315-342.
Shurkin, J. N. (1992). *Terman's kids: The groundbreaking study of how the gifted grow up.* Boston: Little, Brown.
Sicola, P. K. (1990). Where do gifted students fit? An examination of middle school philosophy as it relates to ability grouping and the gifted learner. *Journal for the Education of the Gifted, 14*, 37-49.
Silverman, L. K. (1989). The highly gifted. In J. Feldhusen, J. Van Tassel-Baska, & K. Seeley (Eds.), *Excellence in educating the gifted* (pp. 71-83). Denver: Love.
Silverman, L. K., & Kearney, K. (1989). Parents of the extraordinarily gifted. *Advanced Development Journal, 1*(1), 41-56.

Smith, J., LeRose, B., & Clasen, R. E. (1991). Underrepresentation of minority students in gifted programs: Yes! It matters! *Gifted Child Quarterly, 35,* 81-83.

Smith, T. E. (1992). Gender differences in the scientific achievement of adolescents: Effects of age and parental separation. *Social Forces, 71,* 469-484.

Spicker, H. H. (1992). Identifying and enriching rural gifted children. *Educational Horizons, 70*(2), 60-65.

Stanley, J. C. (1977). Rationale of the Study of Mathematically Precocious Youth (SMPY) during its first five years of promoting educational acceleration. In J. C. Stanley, W. C. George, & C. H. Solano (Eds.), *The gifted and the creative: A fifty-year perspective* (pp. 75-112). Baltimore, MD: Johns Hopkins University Press.

Stanley, J. C. (1991). Critique of "Socioemotional adjustment of adolescent girls enrolled in a residential acceleration program." *Gifted Child Quarterly, 35,* 67-70.

Steinberg, A., & Wheelock, A. (1992). After tracking—what? Middle schools find new answers. *Harvard Education Letter, 8*(5), 1-4.

Sternberg, R. J. (1990). T & T is an explosive combination: Technology and testing. *Educational Psychologist, 25,* 201-222.

Stone, E. (1992). *The Hunter College Campus Schools for the Gifted: The challenge of equity and excellence.* New York: Teachers College Press.

Storfer, M. D. (1990). *Intelligence and giftedness: The contributions of heredity and early environment.* San Francisco: Jossey-Bass.

Strom, R., Johnson, A., Strom, S., & Strom, P. (1992). Educating gifted Hispanic children and their parents. *Hispanic Journal of Behavioral Sciences, 14,* 383-393.

Strum, C. (1993, April 1). Schools' tracks and democracy—Sorting students by performance: Efficiency or elitism? *The New York Times,* pp. B1, B7.

Supplee, P. L. (1990). *Reaching the gifted underachiever.* New York: Teachers College Press.

Tallent-Runnels, M. K., & Martin, M. R. (1992). Identifying Hispanic gifted children using the Screening Assessment for Gifted Elementary Students. *Psychological Reports, 70,* 939-942.

Tannenbaum, A. J. (1983). *Gifted children: Psychological and educational perspectives.* New York: Macmillan.

Tannenbaum, A. J. (1992). Early signs of giftedness: Research and commentary. *Journal for the Education of the Gifted, 15,* 104-133.

Teaching inequality. (1989). [Note]. *Harvard Law Review, 102,* 1318-1341.

Terman, L. M. (1925). *Genetic studies of genius* (Vol. 1). Stanford, CA: Stanford University Press.

Terman, L. M., & Oden, M. (1947). *Genetic studies of genius* (Vol. 4). Stanford, CA: Stanford University Press.

The tracking wars: Is anyone winning? (1992). *Harvard Education Letter, 8*(3), 1-4.
Thorkildsen, T. A. (1993). Those who can, tutor: High-ability students' conceptions of fair ways to organize learning. *Journal of Educational Psychology, 85,* 182-190.
Thorndike, E. L. (1920). Intelligence and its uses. *Harper's, 140,* 227-235.
Thurstone, L. L. (1938). *Primary mental abilities.* Chicago: University of Chicago Press.
Tinajero, J. V. (1992, Winter). Raising educational and career aspirations of Hispanic girls and their mothers. *Journal of Educational Issues of Language Minority Students, 11,* 27-43.
Toch, T., Linnon, N., & Cooper, M. (1991, May 27). Schools that work. *Newsweek,* pp. 58-66.
Tomlinson, C. A. (1992). Gifted education and the middle school movement: Two voices on teaching the academically talented. *Journal for the Education of the Gifted, 15,* 206-238.
Tomlinson, C. A., & Callahan, C. M. (1992). Contributions of gifted education to general education in a time of change. *Gifted Child Quarterly, 36,* 183-189.
Tomlinson-Keasey, C. (1990). Developing our intellectual resources for the 21st century: Educating the gifted. *Journal of Educational Psychology, 82,* 399-403.
Torrance, E. P. (1966). *The Torrance tests of creative thinking: Norms-technical manual.* Princeton, NJ: Personnel Press.
Torrance, E. P. (1984). The role of creativity in identification of the gifted and talented. *Gifted Child Quarterly, 28,* 153-156.
Treffinger, D. J. (1986). Research on creativity. *Gifted Child Quarterly, 30,* 15-19.
Tucker, B. F. (1982). Providing for the mathematically gifted child in the regular elementary classroom. *Roeper Review, 4*(4), 11-12.
Tuttle, D. H., & Cornell, D. G. (1993). Maternal labeling of gifted children: Effects on the sibling relationship. *Exceptional Children, 59,* 402-410.
Van Tassel-Baska, J. (1989a). The disadvantaged gifted. In J. Feldhusen, J. Van Tassel-Baska, & K. Seeley (Eds.), *Excellence in educating the gifted* (pp. 53-69). Denver: Love.
Van Tassel-Baska, J. (1989b). The role of the family in the success of disadvantaged gifted learners. *Journal for the Education of the Gifted, 13,* 22-36.
Van Tassel-Baska, J. (1991). Teachers as counselors for gifted students. In R. M. Milgram (Ed.), *Counseling gifted and talented children: A guide for teachers, counselors, and parents* (pp. 37-52). Norwood, NJ: Ablex.

Vonnegut, K., Jr. (1991). Harrison Bergeron. In J. Selzer (Ed.), *Conversations: Readings for writing* (pp. 683-690). New York: Macmillan.

Walker, B. A., & Freeland, T. (1986, Fall). Gifted girls grow up. *Journal of NAWDAC*, pp. 26-32.

Walker, B. A., Reis, S. M., & Leonard, J. S. (1992). A developmental investigation of the lives of gifted women. *Gifted Child Quarterly, 36*, 201-204.

Warner, J. H., & Rosof, P. J. F. (1992, Summer). Making connections: The eighth-grade English and Social Studies curriculum. *Hunter Outreach*, pp. 1, 4.

Wendorf, D. J., & Frey, J., III (1985). Family therapy with the intellectually gifted. *American Journal of Family Therapy, 13*, 31-38.

When bright kids get bad grades. (1992, November/December). *Harvard Education Letter, 8*(6), 1-3.

Whitmore, J. (1985). New challenges to common identification practices. In J. Freeman (Ed.), *The psychology of gifted children* (pp. 93-113). London: John Wiley.

Whitmore, J. R. (1988). Gifted children at risk for learning difficulties. *Teaching Exceptional Children, 20*(4), 10-14.

Winebrenner, S., & Devlin, B. (1993, Winter). Cluster grouping fact sheet: How to provide full-time services for gifted students on existing budgets. *PAGE Update*, pp. 6-7.

Woliver, R., & Woliver, G. M. (1991). Gifted adolescents in the emerging minorities: Asians and Pacific Islanders. In M. Bireley & J. Genshaft (Eds.), *Understanding the gifted adolescent: Educational, developmental, and multicultural issues* (pp. 248-257). New York: Teachers College Press.

Yong, F. L., & McIntyre, J. D. (1991). Comparison of self-concepts of students identified as gifted and regular students. *Perceptual and Motor Skills, 73*, 443-446.

Zigler, E., & Farber, E. A. (1985). Commonalities between the intellectual extremes: Giftedness and mental retardation. In F. D. Horowitz & M. O'Brien (Eds.), *The gifted and talented: Developmental perspectives* (pp. 387-408). Washington, DC: American Psychological Association.

Zorbaugh, H. W., & Boardman, R. K. (1936). Salvaging our gifted children. *Journal of Educational Sociology, 10*, 100-108.

Zorbaugh, H. W., Boardman, R. K., & Sheldon, P. (1951). Some observations of highly gifted children. In P. Witty (Ed.), *The gifted child* (pp. 86-105). Westport, CT: Greenwood.

Name Index

Abbott, J. A., 42, 127
Abra, J., 77-78, 127
Abroms, K. I., 17, 127
Adler, L. L., 136
Albert, R. S., 19, 138
Anastasi, A., 42, 127
Angelou, M., 78
Armour-Thomas, E., 32, 127
Asher, J. W., 13, 131
The Association for the Gifted, 81, 127
Assouline, S. G., 97, 128
Astin, H. S., 70, 77, 127
Ault, M. M., 103, 133
Ayles, R., 68, 127

Baird, Z., 71
Baldwin, A. Y., 36, 127
Barbe, W. S., 137
Barbee, A. H., 109, 139
Barber, B. R., 66, 128
Bardwick, J., 133
Baska, L. K., 17, 26, 29-30, 128
Bathgate, A. J., 62, 128
Beethoven, L. V., 45
Bell, L. A., 71-72, 128
Benbow, C. P., 76, 95-96, 114, 130, 137
Benedict, R., 77
Bentsen, C., 8, 128

Bermúdez, A. B., 37-38, 128, 135
Berry, J. W., 42, 135
Birch, J. W., 14, 128
Bireley, M., 45, 128, 133, 142
Boardman, R. K., 3, 25-26, 142
Bogat, G. A., 100, 128
Boodoo, G. M., 45, 128
Booth, L., 100, 128
Braddock, J. H., 33, 89, 128
Bradley, C. L., 45, 128
Brody, L. E., 97, 128
Brooks, R., 48, 128
Brown, V., 112
Brown, W. K., 53, 128
Bull, B. L., 1, 5, 12, 129
Bush, G., 4
Byrnes, D. A., 47, 137

Callahan, C. M., 4, 69, 76, 124, 129, 141
Carmichael, L., 134
Cassatt, M., 77
Charles, R., 45
Chetelat, F. J., 18, 129
Christensen, P., 33, 134
Christopherson, S. L., 93-94, 129
Churchill, W., 45
Clark, G. A., 105, 129
Clasen, R. E., 117, 140
Clinkenbeard, P. R., 31, 85, 129

143

Clinton, B., 4, 71
Clinton, H. R., 71
Colangelo, N., 33, 134
Colon, P. J., 85, 129
Congressional Record, 9, 129
Connelly, L. A., 62, 128
Cooper, M., 91, 141
Cornell, D. G., 22, 24, 56, 76, 129, 132, 141
Council for Exceptional Children, 81, 127
Cox, A., 5, 129
Cramer, R. H., 125, 129
Cramond, B., 60, 62, 129
Cronbach, L., 108
Cropley, A., 59, 129
Csikszentmihalyi, M. A., 64, 129
Cummings, M. A., 43, 130
Curie, M., 77-78

Daniels, R., 79, 134
Darling-Hammond, L., 128
Davidson, K. L., 43, 130
DeAngelis, T., 124, 130
DeLeon, P. H., 41, 123, 130
Delisle, J. R., 62, 130
DeLong, M. R., 101, 138
Demetrulias, D. M., 62, 130
Devlin, B., 84, 142
Dillon, S., 91, 130
Douvan, E., 133
Dreiser, T., 101
Drummond, J. E., 98, 137

Edlind, E. P., 99, 130
Einstein, A., 12, 45
Erikson, E. H., 21, 130

Farber, E. A., 125, 142
Farley, F., 30, 130
Farmer, H. S., 73, 130
Feagin, J. R., 41, 130
Feldhusen, J. F., 13, 61, 87, 92, 95, 106, 128, 130-131, 134, 139, 141
Feldman, D., 10, 12, 15, 131

Feldman, R. D., 111-112, 131
Festinger, L. A., 95, 131
Feuerstein, R., 33, 131
Firestien, R., 136
Fischman, R., 2, 47, 117, 120, 139
Fishkin, A., 19, 131
Fletcher, G. H., 86, 131
Flynn, J. R., 40, 131
Foley, J. P., Jr., 42, 127
Ford, D. Y., 23, 51-52, 131
Frasier, M. M., 34, 131
Freeland, T., 109-110, 142
Freeman, J., 127, 142
Frey, J., III, 56, 142
Frontera, R. L., 45, 128
Frydman, M., 16, 131

Gallagher, J. J., 2-4, 19, 50-51, 66, 123, 131
Gallucci, N. T., 19, 132
Garcia, R. L., 41, 132
Gardner, H., 11-12, 132, 134
Genshaft, J., 128, 133, 142
George, W. C., 139-140
Gielen, U. P., 136
Gold, S., 39, 139
Goldring, E. B., 82, 87, 136
Gonzalez, A., 39, 137
Griffin, J. B., 34, 132
Griggs, S. A., 26, 62, 132
Gross, M. U. M., 23-24, 96, 98, 132
Grossberg, I. N., 22, 132
Guttman, D., 133

Haensley, P. A., 99, 130
Halpern, D. F., 72, 132
Halsted, J. W., 22, 132
Handel, R. D., 70, 132
Handler, B. S., 77, 139
Harrel, G., 99, 134
Harris, J., III, 23, 131
Harvey, S., 47-48, 132
Hayes, M. L., 62, 132
Heid, M. K., 16, 103, 132
Higham, S. J., 71-72, 132
Hildreth, G. H., 3, 132

Hogan, A., 39, 139
Hoge, R. D., 22, 132
Hollingworth, L. S., 3, 14, 22, 133
Hong, E., 63, 133
Hoover, S. M., 13, 131
Horner, M., 67, 75, 113, 133
Horowitz, F. D., 127, 130, 142
Howard, S. W., 103, 133
Huffman, L. E., 61, 131
Hunter, T., 90

Irvine, S. H., 135
Isaksen, S. G., 136
Isser, N., 40, 133

Janos, P. M., 26, 96, 133, 138
Jenkins-Friedman, R., 51, 134
Johnson, A., 39, 140
Jones, E. D., 97, 130, 133

Kaplan, C., 14, 133
Karnes, F. A., 17, 57, 60, 133
Kaslow, F. W., 57, 133
Katzko, M. W., 127, 136
Kaufmann, F. A., 99-100, 112-113, 133-134
Kearney, K., 5, 139
Keirouz, K. S., 56, 134
Kerr, B., 33, 75, 78, 134
Kerr, B. A., 114-115, 134
Kierstead, F. D., 41, 134
Kimpston, R. D., 83, 98, 138
Kipsett, L., 130
Kitano, M. K., 35, 134
Knowlton, H. E., 103, 133
Kolloff, P. B., 86, 105, 134
Kornhaber, M., 11-12, 100, 134
Krechevsky, M., 11, 134
Kwan, P. C. F., 68, 134

Laffoon, K. S., 51-52, 134
Lamb, J., 79, 134
Lathlaen, P., 60, 134
Leland, C., 70, 77, 127

Lembke, R. C., 67, 134
Leonard, J. S., 109, 142
LeRose, B., 117, 140
Levy, P. S., 5, 134
Lewin, K., 11, 27, 134
Lewis, J. F., 38, 135
Lewis, L. H., 74, 135
Linnon, N., 91, 141
Lovance, K. J., 93, 138
Lowe, B., 50, 138
Loyd, B., 76, 129
Lupkowski, A. E., 94-95, 135
Lynch, S., 104, 135
Lynch, S. J., 58, 135
Lynn, R., 16, 131

Manegold, C. S., 50, 135
Marquardt, R. G., 57, 133
Márquez, J. A., 38, 135
Marsh, H. W., 88, 135
Martin, C. E., 60, 62, 129
Martin, M. R., 38, 140
Matarazzo, J. D., 36, 135
Matthews, M., 84, 135
Maxey, J., 33, 134
McCarney, S. B., 10, 135
McIntyre, J. D., 23, 142
McIntyre, M., 126, 135
McLeod, J., 59, 129
McPartland, J. M., 33, 89, 128
McShane, D. A., 42, 135
McSheffrey, R., 22, 132
Mead, M., 69, 77-78, 135
Mercer, J. R., 38, 135
Meriweather-Bean, S., 17, 133
Merrell, K. W., 43, 130
Middlebrooks, M. W., 87, 135
Midori, 9
Milam, C. P., 99, 134
Milgram, N. A., 136
Milgram, N. C., 85, 135
Milgram, R. M., 5-6, 13, 30, 63, 82, 87, 106, 116, 132-133, 135-136, 139, 141
Miller, J., 99, 134
Mills, C. J., 58, 104, 135
Minner, S., 45, 136

Mitchell, B. M., 6, 136
Mitchell, M., 77
Mitnick, L. L., 130
Monks, F. J., 6, 27, 136
Moore, A. D., 105, 134
Morisot, B., 77
Mulhern, J. D., 5, 85, 136
Murdock, M. C., 136

Naglieri, J. A., 43, 136
Navarre, J., 71-72, 132, 136
Nelson, J. G., 30, 137
Nelson, K. C., 59, 137
Nielson, A. B., 57, 138
Noble, K. D., 98, 137

O'Brien, M., 127, 130, 142
Oden, M., 50, 140
O'Keeffe, G., 78
Ortiz, V. Z., 39, 137
Osborne, J. K., 47, 137

Pankratz, L. D., 36, 135
Parker, M., 82, 138
Patton, J. M., 36, 137
Perez, G. S., 23, 54, 137
Perlman, I., 45
Perou, R., 39, 139
Perrone, P., 28, 78, 137
Pitts, J. R., 45, 128
Plas, J. M., 42, 135
Pollins, L. D., 95, 114, 137
Prindle, N., 59, 137

Radford, J., 14, 137
Rakow, S. J., 37-38, 128, 135
Ramsay, A., 94, 135
Redding, R. E., 50, 137
Redner, R. L., 100, 128
Reis, S. M., 9, 85, 109, 137, 142
Renzulli, J. S., 9, 15, 36, 61, 85-86, 137
Rhodes, W. A., 53, 128
Richardson, T. M., 76, 94-96, 114, 138

Rimm, S. B., 51, 93, 138
Robinson, N. M., 26, 96, 133, 138
Rogers, J. A., 57, 138
Rogers, K. B., 13, 83, 98, 138
Roosevelt, E., 78
Rosof, P. J. F., 87, 142
Ross, A., 82, 138
Runco, M. A., 19, 138

Salerno-Sonnenberg, N., 25, 138
Sanfilippo, S. M., 96, 133
Sato, I. S., 81, 138
Sawyer, R. N., 101-102, 138
Schack, G. D., 10, 138
Schneider, S., 49, 138
Schuerger, J. M., 23, 131
Schwartz, L. L., 2, 34, 36, 40, 47, 57, 67, 69, 75, 79, 115, 117, 120, 133, 138-139
Scott, M., 54, 139
Scott, M. S., 39-40, 139
Sears, P. S., 108-109, 139
Sears, R., 108
Seeley, K., 46, 48, 59, 61-62, 127, 139, 141
Seeley, K. R., 47-48, 132
Selzer, J., 142
Shanker, A., 124, 139
Shaw, E. L., 62, 129
Sheldon, P., 26, 142
Shmurak, C. B., 77, 139
Shurkin, J. N., 29, 109, 139
Sicola, P. K., 82, 139
Sills, B., 78
Silverman, L. K., 14, 55, 139
Sloat, R. S., 62, 132
Smith, J., 117, 140
Smith, T. E., 57, 74, 140
Solano, C. H., 139-140
Southern, W. T., 97, 130, 133
Spicker, H. H., 44, 140
Stanley, J. C., 97, 114, 125, 128, 130, 137, 139-140
Starko, A. J., 10, 138
Stein, G., 78
Steinberg, A., 90, 140
Sternberg, R. J., 12, 105, 140

Stone, E., 76, 90, 140
Storfer, M. D., 125, 140
Strom, P., 39-40, 140
Strom, R., 39-40, 140
Strom, S., 39-40, 140
Strong, J. H., 87, 135
Strum, C., 66, 140
Supplee, P. L., 51, 84, 140
Swall, R. A., 103, 133

Tallent-Runnels, M. K., 38, 140
Tannenbaum, A., 12, 15, 140
Tannenbaum, A. J., 9-10, 86, 140
Terman, L. M., 3, 22, 29, 50, 107-109, 111, 140
Thorkildsen, T. A., 84, 141
Thorndike, E. L., 17, 141
Thurstone, L. L., 12, 141
Tinajero, J. V., 55, 141
Toch, T., 91, 141
Tollefson, N., 51, 134
Tomlinson, C. A., 4, 122, 124, 141
Tomlinson-Keasey, C., 4, 141
Torrance, E. P., 18-19, 46, 141
Treffinger, D. J., 19, 85, 129, 136, 141
Truman, H. S., 112
Tucker, B. F., 5, 141
Tuttle, D. H., 56, 141

Urbano, R., 39, 139

Valentine-French, S., 77-78, 127

VanBoxtel, H. W., 127, 136
VandenBos, G. R., 41, 123, 130
Van Tassel-Baska, J., 34, 54, 62, 128, 139, 141
von Brock, A. B., 101, 138
Vonnegut, K., Jr., 66, 124, 142

Wagner, P. A., Jr., 41, 134
Walker, B. A., 109-110, 142
Warner, J. H., 87, 142
Watson, J. D., 112
Wendorf, D. J., 56, 142
Wheelock, A., 90, 140
Whiston, S. C., 63, 133
Whitmore, J., 46, 50, 142
Whitmore, J. R., 49, 54, 58, 61, 142
Whitmore, M., 94, 135
Whorton, J. E., 60, 133
Williams, W. G., 6, 136
Winebrenner, S., 84, 142
Woliver, G. M., 40-41, 63, 142
Woliver, R., 40-41, 63, 142
Wooddell, G. D., 86, 131
Woody, P. H., 135
Woolverton, N., 99, 134
Wright, L. B., 45, 128

Yong, F. L., 23, 142

Zigler, E., 125, 142
Zimmerman, E. D., 105, 129
Zorbaugh, H. W., 3, 25-26, 142

Subject Index

A Better Chance, 34

Black Intelligence Test of Cultural Homogeneity (BITCH), 36

Characteristics of the gifted:
  above-average abilities, 9, 14, 20
  creativity, 9-10, 18-20, 37-38, 44, 46, 48, 50, 71, 77-78, 112
  intellectual curiosity, 17, 28, 30, 38, 48, 71
  leadership, 17, 26, 47, 91
  learning style, 13, 26, 51, 100
  leisure activities, 13, 30, 116, 120
  locus of control, 28, 45, 51, 74-75, 121
  memory, 39, 46, 111
  problem-solving, 14, 19, 30
  task committment, 9, 13, 26, 37, 42, 54, 112, 121
  type T personality, 30
College-related special programs:
  Clarkson School, 94
  Cullowhee Experience, 105
  "Discovery" Program, 104
  Duke University's By-Mail Program, 101-102
  Early Entrance Program (EEP), 94, 96-98

Gifted at Ogontz, 117-120
Gifted Education Resource Institute, 94
Johns Hopkins Center for Talented Youth, 57, 104, 107
Math Options, 57, 104, 107
Mother-Daughter Program, 55
Program for the Exceptionally Gifted, 94
Simon's Rock-Bard College Program, 94
Study of Mathematically Precocious Youth (SMPY), 94-95, 97, 113-114
Texas Academy of Math and Science (TAMS), 94-96
University of Pennsylvania, 104
University of Texas at El Paso, 55, 57
University of Virginia, 24, 56
Yale Summer Psychology Program, 105

DOVE Counter-Balance Intelligence Test, 36

"Education 2000," 4-5
Education for All Handicapped Children Act of 1975, 3

Subject Index

Equal educational opportunities, 1, 5-6, 64

Fear of failure, 25, 31, 41, 51, 67-68, 75
Fear of success, 24, 31, 41, 67-68, 75
4x4 Structure of Giftedness, 13

Gender differences, 68, 72-73, 77, 108, 113
Gifted and Talented Children's Act, 8

Identification criteria, 9, 13
  accomplishment self-report, 19
  checklists, 36
  grades, 10, 20, 92
  IQ scores, 9-11, 13, 20, 28
  multimodal assessment, 10-11, 13, 36
  nomination, 11, 16-17, 36, 47-48, 57
  observation, 18, 47
  problem-solving ability, 19-20
  structured interview, 11
  student portfolios, 11, 18, 91
  vocabulary, 10, 14
Individualized Education Programs (IEPs), 2, 46, 62, 81

Mentors, 55, 60, 77, 82-83, 87, 99-101, 110

National Association for Gifted Children (NAGC), 61

"Palcuzzi Ploy", 2, 19
Peer relations, 22-24, 28, 51-52, 58-59, 68, 70, 81, 105, 109, 123-124
Presidential scholars, 99, 112-113
Psychosocial development, 21-22, 62

Role models, 23, 70-71, 74, 77-78, 99, 110

Satellite Educational Resources Consortium (SERC), 103
School-related programs:
  advanced placement courses, 93, 97, 102
  CHALLENGE Program, 100
  curriculum compacting, 85
  governor's Schools of Excellence, 104
  integrative acceleration, 95
  Milford Futurology Program, 86
  National Law Camp, 105
  "Olympics of the Mind", 31
  Program for Academic and Creative Enrichment (PACE), 86-87
  Skills Reinforcement Project, 57, 104
  Summer Institute for the Gifted, 104
  Tracking, 2, 65-66, 89-90
  U.S. Space and Rocket Center, 105
Self-concept, 22-24, 76, 82, 95, 105, 123
Special education for the gifted, 1-2, 6, 95, 125
Special schools:
  Bronx High School of Science, 91
  Central High School, 91
  Hunter College Elementary School, 90
  Hunter College High School, 76, 109-111
  LaGuardia High School of Music and Art, 91
  Masterman School, 91
  Montgomery Blair High School, 91
  Philadelphia High School for Girls, 91
  Trotter Elementary School, 91
Standardized tests:
  Baldwin's Identification Matrix, 36
  Bilingual examiners, 34
  Coopersmith Self-Esteem Inventory, 95-96
  Gifted Evaluation Scale, 10

Kaufman Assessment Battery for Children (K-ABC), 36, 43
Mathematics Attitude Inventory, 79
Parent as a Teacher Inventory, 39
Piers-Harris Children's Self-Concept Scale, 23
Primary Mental Abilities, 12
Rorschach Psychodiagnostic, 20
Scholastic Aptitude Test, 94
Screening Assessment for Gifted Elementary Students, 38
Self-Perception Profile for Children, 22
Stanford-Binet Intelligence Test, 12, 14
Strong-Campbell Vocational Interest Inventory, 78
Structure of Intellect (SOI) Tests, 39
System of Multicultural Pluralistic Assessment (SOMPA), 38
Tel-Aviv Activities Inventory, 63
Torrance Tests of Creative Thinking, 36, 39, 47
Triarchic Abilities Test, 12
Wechsler Scales of Intelligence, 12, 14, 38-39, 42-43, 47
Wide Range Achievement Test (WRAT), 47
Teachers of the Gifted, 59-62, 70, 85, 124
The Association for the Gifted (TAG), 61
Confratute, 61
Creative Problem-Solving Institute, 61-62
National Board for Professional Teaching Standards, 60
National/State Leadership Training Institute on the Gifted and Talented (N/S LTI), 61
Types of giftedness:
  academically gifted, 14, 18, 30, 83
  artistically gifted, 18, 22, 77-78, 85
  disadvantaged gifted, 33-34
  learning disabled gifted, 45
  profoundly gifted, 13, 55
  socially gifted, 17-18, 20
  socioeconomically disadvantaged gifted, 54-55, 117

Westinghouse Science Talent Search, 31, 92

In compliance with GPSR, should you have any concerns about the safety of this product, please advise: International Associates Auditing & Certification Limited The Black Church, St Mary's Place, Dublin 7, D07 P4AX Ireland EUAR@ie.ia-net.com